P9-AGS-414

Literature Online

Reading & Internet Activities for Libraries & Schools

Karen A. Moran

Alleyside Press

Fort Atkinson, Wisconsin

Published by Alleyside Press,
an imprint of Highsmith Press LLC
Highsmith Press
W5527 Highway 106
P.O. Box 800
Fort Atkinson, Wisconsin 53538-0800
1-800-558-2110

© Copyright by Karen A. Moran, 1999
Cover design: Frank Neu

The paper used in this publication meets the minimum requirements of American National
Standard for Information Science — Permanence of Paper for Printed Library Material.
ANSI/NISO Z39.48-1992.

Library of Congress Cataloging-in-Publication Data
    Moran, Karen, 1952-
      Literature online : reading & Internet activities for schools &
   libraries / Karen A. Moran.
      p. cm.
     Includes bibliographical references.
     ISBN 1-57950-032-3 (pbk. : alk. paper)
     1. Children's literature--Study and teaching (Elementary)--United
  States. 2. Internet (Computer network) in education--United States.
  3. Language arts (Elementary)--United States--Computer-assisted
  instruction. I. Title.
   LB1575.5.U5 .M67 1999
   372.64 ' 044--dc21
                                            99-21415
                                               CIP

Contents

Link for *Literature Online*
www.hpress.highsmith.com/kamup.htm

Introduction

Literature Online: Reading & Internet Activities for Libraries & Schools encourages teachers and librarians to utilize the World Wide Web as a valuable resource in the classroom and for library programs. The purpose of Literature Online is to connect children's literature with other areas of the curriculum by using Internet websites and teacher-directed activities, and to provide creative suggestions for use by children's librarians and school media specialists to enhance reading programs using Internet resources.

Specific websites are used as catalysts for activities which cover all areas of the curriculum—language arts, science, social studies, math, art, music, and health. Students are asked to respond to the literature by completing website activities which require them to use:

- writing skills,
- listening skills,
- problem-solving skills,
- math computation,
- higher order thinking skills,
- oral communication,
- creative expression, and
- comprehension skills.

How to Use This Book

Literature Online provides websites and cross-curricular activities for 38 popular children's literature books with reading/interest levels for children ages 8–12 (grades 4–8). After reading one of the selected titles, a student can be referred to the websites chosen for that particular book. The student can then be directed to complete activities using the information located on the designated Web pages.

Format of the Website Activity Pages

The books are listed in alphabetical order by title. Each is introduced with the bibliographic citation, an approximate reading level, and a short summary. However, the determination of a reading level is not an exact science. Reading levels will vary throughout a book depending upon the passages which are chosen for examination. Use your own judgment when deciding which books are suitable for your classroom or library program.

Websites

Site name and URL (address) are given with a brief description of the site and the name of the sponsoring agency or webmaster. To make use of the sites you choose easier, we provide a downloadable file with site names and URLs at the **H Link** page for *Literature Online* <www.hpress. highsmith.com/kamup.htm.

The sites were chosen based on the following criteria:

1. Organization—Is the site well organized and easy for the teacher and student to navigate? It should not be cluttered with links, directions, graphics, or advertisements.

2. Stability—Is the site maintained by a reliable host or provider?

3. Safe-site—Is the site age-appropriate for the students? It must not contain objectionable information.

4. Cross-curricular—Does the site include material which may be found in the grade 4-8 curriculum? A literature-based website was chosen for each book whenever possible.

Website Activities

The activities are fun, educational, and cross-curricular. The directions are concisely written and the vocabulary is geared to the reading level of each individual book. Many of the activities challenge students to use higher order thinking skills. You may wish to identify additional websites and create your own activities to meet the needs of your students and your curriculum. For information on conducting your own search and for updating the websites in the book, see chapter 2.

How to Use the Website Activities

Always bookmark the websites ahead of time. This will reduce time spent in searching for the sites and allow you to test activities and check for changes or modifications in the websites. There are a variety of ways to use the website activities. The following is a list of suggestions:

Read portions of the book together as a library program or class project. Have students work individually, with a partner, or in small groups to complete the website activities.

Have students work independently by selecting their own books and completing the corresponding Internet activities.

Assign a book to a group of students. Ask them to read the story together and complete the website activities as a team.

Read the story together as a group. Introduce the websites using either an LCD panel and overhead projector or an LCD video projector with Internet access. Have the students complete the activities individually.

Useful Web Utilities

Some website activities require you to use specific software utilities. It may be beneficial to have the following utilities downloaded to your computer: Shockwave, Quick Time, Real Audio, and Real Player.

Super Search

Super Search questions require the student to locate a specific answer on the designated Web pages. Super Search questions may be used in the classroom as extra-credit or free-time activities, homework, or for enhancing library programs. The answers to all Super Search questions are in the back of this book.

On Your Own

A list of discussion topics is included for each book featured in *Literature Online*. This list is provided for teachers, librarians, and students who wish to conduct their own searches for additional websites and activities.

Suggested Reading

A list of additional titles written by the same author or books written on a similar theme is included to aid in further enriching library programs and classroom activities.

Additional Sources

This section of the book includes educational multimedia resources which provide additional information on the subject matter found in each of the featured titles in *Literature Online*.

Chapter One

Providing for Individual Differences

There is a wide disparity in the ability levels among the children in any given class. This chapter addresses how to accommodate for individual differences among students. Alternative approaches and suggestions are given for gifted/enrichment students and for students who have learning difficulties.

Of course, the following strategies and suggestions need not be used exclusively with gifted/ enrichment students. Whenever possible, adapt the activities and encourage *all* students to use higher order thinking skills.

Suggestions for Gifted/Enrichment Students

• Have students select their own books based upon their individual reading and interest levels. Students may complete the website activities independently as a free-time or extra credit activity.

• Have students search for additional websites by using the key search words listed in the "On Your Own" section for each book featured in *Literature Online*.

• Provide students with the "Suggested Reading" and "Additional Sources" listed after each set of website activities. The students should:

   compare and contrast books written by the same author, or
   compare and contrast books written on a similar theme.

• Then list connections they can make between the information in the fiction and nonfiction titles written on the same topic.

• Encourage oral communication.

• Direct students to create plays by dramatizing a scene from the book. Tell students to make the setting, plot, and characters authentic by searching websites for relevant details to include in the context of the play.

• Have students prepare an informative speech using material found in a web search.

• Develop computer skills and information skills used in searching the Web.

• Assist students in creating a Web page which features:

   a summary of the book,
   biographical information on the author, and
   a critic's review section with comments from your students.

• Encourage students to become student facilitators by providing them with strategies for helping others with basic computer skills or web-related searches.

• Direct students to use their Web research to complete the following projects:

   Develop a cultural diversity program which provides information on multi-ethnic dances, foods, customs, etc.
   Create posters, bulletin boards, or learning centers for the classroom.
   Search for additional Super Search questions and use the information to make a class trivia game.

• Encourage co-operation and develop problem solving skills by having students brainstorm ideas for a community-service project. They should use information from both their selected book and their Internet research to suggest a project to serve the community or school. For example:

   After the Dancing Days Plan a Veterans' Appreciation Day Program for local veterans in the community.

Owls in the Family   Start a fundraiser to provide money for the local SPCA or promote the adoption of unwanted pets.

Ribsy   Design a pamphlet of fire prevention tips for community residents.

Special note: These projects should be student-generated. The teacher or librarian should only provide guidance and assistance when necessary.

Suggestions for Students with Learning Difficulties

• Be sure the student knows how to use the computer by providing a lesson on basic computer terminology—see appendix A, p. 93. Instruct students on the proper use of computers, emphasizing your classroom rules for using the Internet.

• Provide more detailed instruction for the website activities. Write the directions in steps with an accompanying checklist for the students to follow.

• Use an audiotaped version of the book for students who cannot read the text in the books. Students may use these tapes to "follow along" in the book while they are listening to the audiocassette. Look for information on locating audiotaped versions of books in the following places:

in the Additional Sources sections at the end of each book activity

on the Internet at amazon.com, borders.com, or barnesandnoble.com

at your local library or bookstore.

• Allow students to subvocalize or read quietly when reading information from the websites. Many times students will comprehend better if they can hear what they are reading.

• Select websites which have multimedia capabilities such as the following:

videos,

audio clips,

interactive games—Shockwave, Java.

• Alter the specific directions for a website activity. For example, if the activity directs students to write an essay comparing two characters or situations, have the student list the comparisons.

• Have students keep a journal of facts they have learned from their Web searches. This strategy assists students in transferring data from the computer to print.

• Instruct students to write a rough draft on paper if they are required to send an e-mail message or a response on the computer. Assist students in editing the draft before they post it to the Internet.

• Partner the students with facilitators (peers, parent volunteers, aids, older students).

Chapter Two

Updating Websites and Conducting Your Own Search

Internet websites are constantly changing. Providers may choose not to maintain a site or may move the site to a different location by changing the URL. Although stability was one of the criteria used to select the websites in this resource book, some of the chosen sites will inevitably disappear or move. To update websites in this book, use the 🔗 **Link** at <www.hpress. highsmith.com/kamup.htm>. All changes will be listed there. If a website is no longer available, an alternate site with activities will be provided.

If you are interested in locating sites for a title which is not featured in this book, consider the following steps. You may also wish to use these steps if you prefer to locate additional sites for the books featured in *Literature Online*.

Steps for Conducting Your Own Successful Search

Select a suitable children's literature book.
Choose a book which is age-appropriate for your students and is geared to your students' interest level. Don't be too concerned about the reading level of a book. If the theme is interesting to the students, they will be motivated to read a book even if it is not on their independent reading level.

As you read the book, keep a list of topics which appear in the book. Use the following topics to assist you with searchable ideas:

famous people, scientific terms, historical dates, geographical locations, government agencies, health issues, zoos/aquariums, types of music, advertisements, religions, newspapers, games/puzzles, sports, environment, historical events, cultural events, animals, ethnic customs, art museums, physical fitness, literature genres, manufacturing companies, youth organizations, holidays and traditions, magazines, hobbies, entertainment, food

Select a search engine.
Each engine has a different set of specifications for accessing its database. Some engines are directories with cataloged sites. Other engines include only indexes.

Become familiar with a few of the engines and choose the one(s) you feel most comfortable using. The following is a list of popular search engines:

Alta Vista <http://www.altavista.com>

Excite <http://www.excite.com>

Hot Bot <http://www.hotbot.com/>

InfoSeek <http://www.infoseek.com/>

Web Crawler <http://www.webcrawler.com/>

Yahoo <http://www.yahoo.com/>

*Yahooligans <http://www.yahooligans.com/>
special note—Yahooligans is an excellent engine. It provides a large database of "safe sites" for kids. The sites are categorized and a brief description is given for each site.

Begin your search.
Begin your search with the names of the author and illustrator of the book. Many authors and illustrators have created their own home pages. The home pages usually provide biographical information on the author/illustrator. Activities and links are often given at these sites. Search for the title of the book. This search may lead you to reviews of the book written by individual students or classrooms which have read the book as a project.

Search for book awards your book may have received. These sites may link you to literature-based sites with activities and ideas.

Search for the topics on the list you created while you were reading the book.

As you are searching these topics, think about how you can integrate a particular site into your curriculum.

Bookmark every site you find. Create a new folder for the bookmarked sites. Use the title of the book for the name of the folder. This will help you to quickly locate the site in the future. Even if you do not wish to use a site, bookmark it anyway. You may find later that the site contains valuable links to other useful sites.

Use the "On Your Own" section if you are seeking additional sites for a book featured in Literature Online.

Evaluating websites.

The following criteria may be used to assist you with your website selections:

Age appropriate—The content and reading level of the material is appropriate for your students.

Good design—The material is well-organized and easy for your children to navigate independently. Directions are easy to understand and the text is not too cluttered or wordy.

Accurate—Information provided at the site is reliable and is provided by a reputable authority or organization. the content is clearly stated and is unbiased. The information provided is current.

Safe links—Links at the site do not lead the students to objectionable information on other sites.

Additional information on website evaluation is provided at the following websites:

Critical Evaluations Survey by Kathy Schrock
www.capecod.net/schrockguide/eval.htm

CyberGuides—A Rating System by Karen McLachlan
www.cyberbee.com/guides.html

Library Selection Criteria for WWW Resources by Carolyn Caywood
www.keele.ac.uk/depts/cs/Stephen_Bostock/Internet/criteria.htm

Create appropriate activities to accompany the sites you have chosen.

Vary the activities to include as many areas of your curriculum as possible.

Vary the activities to provide for individual differences among your students. (See chapter 1.)

Chapter Three

Using Children's Literature and Website Activities to Enhance Curriculum

Educators are under increasing pressure to improve achievement scores, use computer technology, and integrate subject matter across the curriculum. Integrating literature into the curriculum using Internet websites serves to meet many of these demands. Internet activities can energize your reading program and enhance your curriculum. School and children's librarians can contribute to this effort by adapting these activities for library skills instruction and reading programs.

The selection of websites for a children's book will depend upon the topics included in the story, the grade level of your students, and your curriculum. The key to using website activities is to correlate themes and events taken from the literature with topics which meet the specific needs of your curriculum. Searching for sites is not difficult once you have identified the topics you will use.

The Process

The following are step-by-step directions on how you can use website activities in each area of your curriculum. *Dragonwings* is used as the example.

1. **Read the book.**

   Dragonwings by Laurence Yep (HarperCollins, 1975). Summary: Moon Shadow's father lives in San Francisco and works in a laundry trying to save enough money to send for his wife and son in China. When Moon Shadow turns eight years old, he sails from China to join his father. The father is obsessed with thoughts of flying and he engages Moon Shadow in his dream of building an airplane. The two Chinese Americans have a difficult time dealing with their Chinese countrymen who ridicule them for following their dream.

2. **Create a list of topics discussed in the book.**

   Chinese customs, Chinese alphabet, Chinese calendar, Wright Brothers, constellations, kites, dirigibles, abacuses, dragons, earthquakes, Chinatown, San Francisco cable cars, stereopticons, hang gliding, airplanes

3. **Determine curriculum areas that match your list.**

   art, health/physical education, math, music, science, social studies

4. **Select at least one website for each area of your curriculum and write activities to correlate with the websites.**

Sample Website Activities for Dragonwings

Art

Take a virtual field trip to a Chinese art gallery.

Find directions for making a paper airplane and have an airplane flying contest in your class. Compare/contrast artwork from two different Chinese dynasties.

Design a travel brochure for San Francisco, California.

Health/Physical Education

Find the proper techniques for successful kite flying.

Locate information on the martial arts.

List the health benefits of eating tofu and soy products.

Language Arts

Read the story of Daedalus and Icarus and compare it with the story of *Dragonwings*. Explain the use of Chinese astrological signs. List Windrider's character traits and determine which astrological sign you think would have been his.

Write a short biography of Laurence Yep and tell why you think he wrote *Dragonwings*.

Recall events from the story which involved the Wright Brothers. Decide which events were fictional.

Read a Chinese folktale and discuss the moral of the story. Compare this moral with the theme of *Dragonwings*.

Find an online newspaper. Search the archives of the newspaper and read an article about earthquakes.

Practice making Chinese characters found in the Chinese alphabet.

Math

Make a time line to portray the chronological events in the lives of the Wright Brothers.

Find a Chinese board game, such as Mancala, and describe the rules of play for the game.

Prepare a chart, graph, or table to report the percentages of Chinese Americans living in Chinatowns throughout the United States.

Design a blueprint for a flying machine. Include the dimensions.

Music

Research popular music of the early 1900s in America.

Discuss the role music played in Chinese culture in the early 1900s.

Science

Visit the NASA website and see how flight has changed since the time of the Kitty Hawk flight.

Take a virtual field trip to a science museum to see the latest inventions.

Learn which stars have been discovered since Moon Shadow studied the constellations in 1906.

Find a picture of a stereopticon and tell how it has evolved.

Read about other earthquakes which occurred in San Francisco, California.

View an image of a San Francisco cable car and explain how it works.

Social Studies

Take a virtual field trip to the Air and Space Museum, Smithsonian Institute in Washington, DC.

Visit the Federal Aviation Administration site and read the regulations for obtaining a pilot's license.

Study Chinese customs and tell which ones are still being celebrated today in China and in America.

Discuss the history of dragons and their importance in the Chinese culture.

Make a map for the route Moon Shadow took when he traveled from China to San Francisco.

Chapter Four

Tips for Kids
Smart Surfing in the Classroom and Library

When you introduce your students to the Internet and explain the website activities, you will probably find a wide range in the level of computer literacy among your students. Some may already be quite adept at using the Internet, others may not even be familiar with basic computer terminology. Establishing a clear set of classroom or library guidelines for Internet use will give both sets of students a framework for using the web to create a rich learning environment.

The guidelines or rules you establish for your setting should be designed with student needs and level of knowledge in mind as well as computer access and availability of resources. The rules for your classroom or library may need to be more stringent depending upon your library or school district's computer policy. Post the rules near the computers so they can be referred to when necessary.

If you are concerned about safe-surfing in your library or classroom, consider having each individual student and his/her parent(s) co-sign a contract which includes a list of the classroom computer rules. The contract may also serve to reassure parents who may be skeptical about their children surfing the World Wide Web in school or the library.

There are software programs called "filters" that are commercially available, and which claim they can block access to objectionable sites. Some libraries and school districts require filters on computers used by children. Tests have shown that filters do not always work. The American Library Association has adopted a policy against the use of filters. This is an issue which is very controversial and policies will differ from one community to another.

The following list is a sample of tips you may wish to consider when developing your own list of rules:

Tips for Kids: Smart Surfing in the Classroom and the Library

Stay on the websites bookmarked by your teacher or librarian unless you are given permission to "surf" for other sites.

Never give your name, address, phone number, teacher's name, or school's name to anyone you meet on the Internet.

Never download a program from the Internet unless your computer is protected with an anti-virus program.

Don't believe everything you read online. Some people may not be telling you the truth.

Never agree to keep a relationship on the Internet secret.

Tell your teacher or librarian if anyone on the Internet asks you to meet them in person. Never make arrangements to meet a stranger.

Never reply to e-mail messages from strangers.

Get permission from your teacher or librarian before you do any of the following:

> Fill out an on-line survey.
>
> Enter a contest.
>
> Send e-mail.
>
> Submit information to a site.
>
> Enter a chat room.
>
> Download a file or program.

Be polite when you send messages. Do not curse or use name-calling.

Tell your teacher or librarian immediately if you see anything on the Internet which seems strange or upsetting.

Literature Books and Website Activities

Abel's Island
William Steig • Collins, 1976
Reading Level: 5.2 • 119 pages

Summary

Abel the Mouse is swept away in a rainstorm while trying to retrieve his wife's scarf. He is stranded on an island for a year and is unaccustomed to fending for himself because he has been raised in a life of leisure. Abel manages to survive and return home to his lovely mouse wife.

Website Activities

1. Niagra Falls

www.niagaraparks.com/attract-idx.html

The Niagara Parks Commission produces this website listing all of the major attractions at Niagra Falls, including transportation suggestions.

Activities

From Abel's perspective, the waterfall he was swept down must have seemed like Niagara Falls. Take a virtual tour of the Canadian side of Niagara Falls. Select three attractions you would like to visit. Then use the attraction rates to estimate how much your trip would cost. (For a special challenge—see if you can convert the cost into U.S. dollars.) **[Math]**

Select "Niagara Parks People Mover" and view the route the People Mover takes through the Falls area. Create an imaginary city and draw a People Mover's route through your city. Add attractions along the route by drawing a picture for each attraction and numbering each one. Make a list of the numbered attractions and describe each one. **[Social Studies]**

Super Search: How much money would you save per child (6–12 years old) if you purchased the Explorer's Passport Plus instead of purchasing a separate admission for each attraction?

2. Super Bridge

www.pbs.org/wgbh/nova/bridge/

This interactive website allows you to learn and test your knowledge about four kinds of bridges. Links to additional sites. Presented by Nova Online, sponsored by PBS and the WGBH Educational Foundation.

Activity

Abel could have used the ideas at this site when he tried to build a bridge to cross the river. Select "Build a Bridge" and read the descriptions of each of the four types of bridges used today. When you are finished, play the game to test your knowledge on bridge construction. Which type of bridge should Abel have built to cross the river? **[Science]**

Super Search: Which bridge is the easiest to construct?

3. Look, Learn, and Do

www.looklearnanddo.com/documents/home.html

The Look, Learn, and Do site is a place where kids can read books, learn interesting historical facts, and build projects with easy to follow, illustrated plans. This site is produced by a team led by Professor Mark Icanberry whose goal is to provide a clean, easy-to-use site for the whole family.

Activity

Abel also tried to leave the island by making a sailboat, but he didn't have any luck. Select "Build a Project" and then "Build a Sailboat." Follow the directions at this site to build your own sailboat. If you have a lake or stream near your school, have a sailboat race with the fleet of sailboats built by your classmates. **[Art]**

Super Search: What should you attach to the back of your boat?

4. Dave's Math Tables

www.sisweb.com/math/general/measures.htm

This is a website devoted to providing math tables on general math, algebra, geometry, trigonometry, statistics, calculus, and other advanced topics.

Activity

Abel measured distances in the story by mouse tails. People measure distances in standard and metric terms. Select "Lengths and Distances" and use the table to help create a "Search for Abel" game for your classmates. Hide Abel (a stuffed or paper mouse) in a secret place in your school. Give specific directions and measurements on how to find Abel. See who can find him in the shortest amount of time. **[Math]**

Super Search: How many centimeters are in an inch?

5. Frogland

www.teleport.com/~dstroy/froglnd.shtml

Frogland provides information and artwork on frogs. It is dedicated to the many teachers who are finding new uses for the Internet as a tool for educating youngsters.

Activities

Gower, the elderly frog, almost died when he was washed down the waterfall. Learn how you can help save other frogs. Select "Save Our Frogs" and "What You Can Do." Read the suggestions for how you can keep frogs from becoming an endangered species. Choose one of the suggestions you would be willing to try in order to help save the frogs. Make a list of the specific steps needed to follow through with your plan. **[Science]**

Select "Stupid Frog Jokes" and share your favorite jokes with the class.

Super Search: What percentage of all plants and animals in the world lives in the tropics?

On Your Own

croquet, mice, Niagara Falls, poisonous mushrooms, bridges, catapults, mental telepathy, owls, measurements, harbingers of spring, Canadian geese, frogs, warts, drought

Suggested Reading

Kellog, Steven. *The Island of the Skog.* Dial Books for Young Readers, 1973. Jenny and her mice friends escape city life to live on a deserted island, but they find the island is inhabited by a Skog.

O'Brien, Robert C. *Mrs. Frisby and the Rats of NIMH.* Atheneum, 1971. A poor widowed mouse seeks help for her ill son from a group of highly intelligent, trained laboratory rats.

Pochocki, Ethel. *The Attic Mice.* Dell, 1990. A family of mice invades the "House of the Humans" where they discover useful items which they borrow.

Steig, William. *Amos and Boris.* Farrar, Straus, & Giroux, 1971. A mouse whose life has been saved by a whale, has a chance to reciprocate with a rescue in another unlikely situation.

Additional Sources

Martin, James. *Hiding Out: Camouflage in the Wild.* Crown, 1993. The author explores how animals use camouflage to survive in their environments.

McCauley, Jane R. *Animals and Their Hiding Places.* National Geographic Society, 1986. Jane McCauley describes places where animals seek shelter and safety for themselves and their young.

2
Across Five Aprils
Irene Hunt • Berkley, 1986
Reading Level: 7.5 • 100 pages

Summary

Jethro is just a young boy who is left to tend the family's potato farm after his father has a heart attack and his brothers go to war. Things get complicated for Jethro when some of the villagers harass him after his brother Bill decides to fight for the Confederacy and his other two brothers go to fight for the Union.

Website Activities

1. Lincoln Boyhood National Memorial

www.nps.gov/libo/index.htm

The National Park Service maintains this site on Lincoln's Boyhood National Monument. It contains basic information for those wishing to tour the memorial.

Activities

Take a virtual field trip to Lincoln's Boyhood National Memorial in southern Indiana. Create a travel brochure for the memorial. Be sure to include information which will be helpful to tourists. Use the directions for "Trails, Roads" to include a map of the three trails in the park.
[Social Studies, Art]

Use the information on admission fees to determine the total price of admission for your entire class if it were to visit the park for a field trip.
[Math]

Super Search: What was Abraham Lincoln's mother's name?

2. Civil War.com

www.civilwar.com

CivilWar.com is sponsored by Premier Internet, Inc. The firm has dedicated itself to providing a resource about the history of the American Civil Ward to students of all ages.

Activity

There were many battles in the Civil War. Select "The Battles." Use the information to make a chart of five of the battles featured at this site. Use the following categories in your chart:

a. Name of battle

b. Location of the battle

c. Date of battle

d. Victor of the battle (Union, Confederate, or Indecisive)

e. Number of casualties   **[Social Studies]**

Super Search: What was the last battle of the war?

3. White House

www2.whitehouse.gov/WH/kids/html/home.html

The official kids home page of the White House. The site includes the following sections: "History of the White House," "Our President," "White House Kids and Pets," and "Write the President."

Activity

Jethro wrote to President Lincoln for advice on how to deal with his situation when he was harboring a Civil War deserter. Select "Write the President." You can send mail to the President, the Vice President, or the First Lady using your computer. If you include your mailing address, you will receive a response. Please have your teacher or parent check your letter before you submit it.
[Language Arts]

Super Search: What was the name of President Lincoln's youngest son?

4. Funbrain

www.funbrain.com/index.html

This is a collection of interactive educational games for children. It is sponsored and published by PM Publishing. This highly acclaimed site has won over twenty awards.

Activity

When Shadrach went to war, he allowed Jethro to keep his grammar books so that Jethro could study. Select "Grammar Gorillas" from the pull down menu and practice your parts of speech by playing this game. When you are finished, select "Spell Check" and choose the hard version to practice your spelling. **[Language Arts]**

Super Search: What is the grammatical term for an outcry or sudden utterance?

5. Eye Witness

www.ibiscom.com/appomatx.htm

Eye Witness recounts history through the words of those who lived it and uses personal narratives and other sources to bring history to life. It is presented by Ibis Communications Inc., a digital publisher of educational CD-ROMs.

Activity

General Lee finally surrendered his troops to General Grant at Appomattox and signed a peace treaty. Read the dispatches sent between the two generals in the final days of the Civil War. Use the information you learned from reading these messages to write a few paragraphs describing how you think each of the Generals felt when they attended the final meeting at Appomattox. **[Social Studies, Language Arts]**

Super Search: In whose house was the treaty signed?

On Your Own

potato farming, Abraham Lincoln, abolitionists, slavery, Fort Sumter, General Grant, General Lee, Tom Paine, Antietam, General McClellan, General Burnside, Confederate Army, Union Army, Appomattox, "Battle Hymn of the Republic," assassinations

Suggested Reading

Bunting, Eve. *The Blue and the Gray.* Scholastic, 1996. A black boy and his white friend watch a house being constructed on the site of a Civil War battlefield.

Hemingway, Edith Morris, and Jacqueline Cosgrove Shields. *Broken Drum.* White Mane, 1996. A twelve-year-old drummer boy in the army is caught in the middle of the Civil War when he travels with the army to Antietam.

Tolliver, Ruby C. *Muddy Banks.* Christian University Press, 1987. A twelve-year-old runaway slave is trapped during the Battle of Sabine Pass when the war threatens to destroy his part of Texas.

Additional Sources

Abraham Lincoln. Arts and Entertainment Audio Books, 1996. Abraham Lincoln's life and history are told on this 100-minute audiocassette.

Across Five Aprils. Random House Video, 1986. This 30-minute VHS contains a guide sheet and is based on the book by Irene Hunt.

Anderson, Nancy Scott, and Dwight Anderson. *The Generals – Ulysses S. Grant and Robert E. Lee.* Knopf, 1987. The Andersons include biographical information about these two leading generals in the Civil War.

Smith, Carter. *1863: The Crucial Year, A Sourcebook on the Civil War.* Milbrook, 1993. Carter Smith uses a variety of materials to explain and illustrate the major events of the Civil War that took place in 1863.

3

After the Dancing Days
Margaret I. Rostkowski • HarperCollins, 1986
Reading Level 5.8 • 217 pages

Summary

Annie's father returns home from World War I and tends to veterans at the local veterans' hospital. Although her mother forbids her to go, Annie makes frequent visits to the hospital and forms a special bond with a disabled soldier who is bitter and withdrawn. Eventually, her mother learns to accept Annie's visits, and Annie convinces her mother to become an advocate for the wounded veterans.

Website Activities

1. The Purple Heart

www.purpleheart.org/explanation.htm

The Military Order of the Purple Heart is an organization for individuals who have been awarded the Purple Heart by the government of the United States of America. This website provides information on the history of the Purple Heart and pertinent facts about the award.

Activity

Andrew received the Purple Heart for being injured in the line of duty, but Annie's uncle did not receive this honor. Annie read as much information as she could about the Purple Heart and why it is awarded. Read the facts on this medal and write a letter to Annie telling her about what you learned from reading the information at this site. **[Language Arts, Social Studies]**

Super Search: Which famous President of the United States created the Purple Heart?

2. Veteran's Facilities Directory

www.va.gov/stations97/guide/home.asp? DIVISION=ALL

Activities

Annie and her family did so much to help their local veterans. Click on the name of your state to view the veterans' facilities in your state. Write a letter to the nearest VA Medical Center or clinic in your area. Ask the administrator for the names of veterans residing at the hospital. Have everyone in your class/school make cards for the patients expressing your gratitude to them for having served in the U.S. armed services. Include a short summary of the book *After the Dancing Days* and explain what you have learned about veterans and how you feel about what they have done for you. **[Art]**

Ask your teacher if you may contact your local veterans' organization or center. Request that a speaker come to your class to speak about what it is like to serve in the military. The addresses and phone numbers for organizations in your state are provided at this site. **[Social Studies]**

Super Search: Find three areas listed at this site that are not states but still have veterans facilities.

3. Tomorrow's Morning

www.morning.com/archives/tm253/historytalk. html

Activity

Tomorrow's Morning is a weekly newspaper for kids (8–14). It is designed to motivate kids to read and understand the issues affecting their lives. The site covers national and international news and also includes features on science, the environment, nature, the stock market, and sports.

Activities

👆 Clara Barton was a famous war nurse during the Civil War. Read this biographical article written on Clara Barton and her accomplishments. Imagine a conversation held between Clara and Annie. Write the words Clara and Annie might have said to each other. Include statements the two women would have made to each other concerning their feelings for the soldiers and the war. **[Language Arts]**

👆 Select "Current Issue" and read the articles in the current issue of Tomorrow's Morning online. Tell whether you would rather read about the news in a newspaper or on the World Wide Web. Write your reasons for making this decision and list the advantages and disadvantages of presenting the news over the Internet.
[Language Arts]

Super Search: What was the name of the relief organization Clara Barton founded?

4. 2216 Baker Street: Sherlock Holmes Consulting Detective

members.tripod.com/~msherman/holmes.html

Michael Sherman is a physicist, computer scientist, and filmmaker who developed this award-winning site titled "221B Baker Street: Sherlock Holmes Consulting Detective." Forty-eight of Arthur Conan Doyle's Sherlock Holmes stories are available at this site.

Activity

👆 Annie's father called her a "Sherlock Holmes" for investigating the reasons why Uncle Paul did not receive a Purple Heart. Sherlock Holmes was a famous detective created by author Sir Arthur Conan Doyle. Doyle wrote 60 mystery stories with Sherlock Holmes as the main character. Read several of the mystery stories available on this site. List five character traits Sherlock Holmes had which made him a successful detective.
[Language Arts]

Super Search: Who was Sherlock Holmes' companion and assistant?

On Your Own

croquet, Red Cross, piano lessons, Harley Davidson, nursing, veterans' hospitals, The Purple Heart, Florence Nightingale, Sherlock Holmes, measles, disabilities, plastic surgery

Suggested Reading

Burnett, Frances (Hodgson). *The Secret Garden.* Dell, 1981. A ten-year-old girl discovers her invalid cousin living in a lonely house on the Yorkshire moors.

DeAngeli, Margurite. *The Door in the Wall.* Dell, 1949. A crippled boy living during the fourteenth century in England earns recognition from the king when he proves how courageous he is.

Hunt, Irene. *Across Five Aprils.* Berkley, 1964. Jethro is left to take care of the family farm in Illinois when his brothers join the army. (See page 22 for activities for this book.)

Riskind, Mary. *Apple Is My Sign.* Houghton Mifflin, 1993. A ten-year-old boy returns home to live on a farm after he spends a year at the Philadelphia School for the Deaf.

Additional Sources

Dolan, Edward F. *America in World War I.* Milbrook, 1996. Edward Dolan presents the history of World War I and the events leading up to the war. He explains the actions of U.S. troops and covers the peace treaty after the war.

The Black Stallion
Walter Farley • Random House, 1941
Reading Level 5.3 • 187 pages

Summary

When his ship is sunk in a storm, Alec is rescued by a wild black stallion. The stallion swims Alec to the shore of a deserted island. Alec learns to communicate with the stallion and they manage to survive together on the island. When they are both rescued, Alec is determined to keep the black stallion and train him to be a race horse.

Website Activities

1. Horse Country

www.horse-country.com/penpals/index.html

"Horse Country" is an international equestrian resource and an interactive community of thousands of kids worldwide.

Activity

If you love horses as much as Alec did, you can communicate with other horse lovers from around the world with Horse Country's International Pen Pals for Kids Program. Before you sign up for a pen pal, get permission from your parent or teacher and then click on the "Important Reminder" to read the warnings about problems you might encounter. **[Language Arts]**

Super Search: What type of letters are considered violations of the United States Federal Law?

2. Breeds of Stock

www.ansi.okstate.edu/breeds/horses/

The Department of Animal Science at Oklahoma State University created this Web page listing the breeds of horses with a description of each individual breed.

Activity

The Black Stallion was an Arabian horse and Alex needed to prove the horse's pedigree by producing official papers on the horse before he could race "The Black." There are almost two hundred breeds of horses in the world. Select one of the breeds at this site and read the facts given about that particular horse. Draw a picture of the horse on a 3x5" index card. Be sure your picture matches the description. Write the characteristics of the horse and other details about the breed on the back of the card. Hang your index card on a bulletin board with the other horse card descriptions your classmates make and you can create a "Classroom Horse Corral " for all the different breeds of horses. If you are ambitious, choose another breed and make an additional card to place in the "corral." **[Science, Art]**

Super Search: How were horses used between 3000 and 4000 BC?

3. Marine Plants and Algae

www.mobot.org/MBGnet/salt/plants/index.htm

The Missouri Botanical Garden LearningNetwork presents this site on Marine Ecosystems. The site is produced and maintained by The Evergreen Project, Inc.

Activity

Alex and the Black Stallion depended on seaweed for nourishment on the island. Read the information about the different types of marine plants found in the ocean. Make a chart with facts for each of the featured algae and marine grasses. Include the following categories in your chart:

1. Name of marine plant

2. Where the plant grows

3. Drawing of the plant

4. Physical characteristics **[Science]**

Super Search: What is the scientific name used for a plant making its own food?

4. International Museum of the Horse

www.imh.org/

This site was developed to provide information on two educational attractions in Lexington, Kentucky — The International Museum of the Horse and the Kentucky Horse Park.

Take a virtual field trip to the International Museum of the Horse. Select the "Virtual Art Galley" and view the exhibitions of photographs and sculptures. Draw four sketches of your favorite events from The Black Stallion. Arrange the sketches in correct sequence as they occurred in the story. Use the information you learn from the website art gallery to create your own classroom "Black Stallion Exhibition" with the sketches completed by your classmates. **[Art]**

Super Search: Which famous sculptor has her work displayed at the art gallery?

5. Horselovers Club

horsefun.com/start.html

The Horselovers Club was originated by a group of Horselovers in Australia. The club created this fun site about horses to keep other horselovers informed and entertained.

Activities

Select "Solve Some Horse Puzzles" and see how many puzzles you can solve at this site. If you solve the "Ultimate Brain Buster," you will get listed on the Brainiac's Page.

Select "Read a Pony Tale" and read the horse story written by a horselover. Create your own horse tale. Use details you learned about horses in your story.

Super Search: What is a male foal called?

On Your Own

horses, stallions, caragheen, seaweed, shipwrecks, horse training, jockeys, Arabians, Kentucky Derby, sportscasters

Suggested Reading

Doty, Jean Slaughter. *If Wishes Were Horses.* Macmillan, 1984. Two children struggle to keep the family horse farm going after their father's death.

Farley, Walter. *The Black Stallion and Satan.* Random House, 1984. The world wonders which stallion is the faster: the great black stallion or his son, Satan.

————. *The Black Stallion Returns.* Random House, 1945. Alec travels across Arabia to find the great stallion after the original owner reclaims the horse.

Sewell, Anna. *Black Beauty.* Grosset and Dunlap, 1945. A nineteenth-century horse in England has experiences with both good and bad masters.

Additional Sources

The Black Stallion Returns. CBX/Fox Video 1984. This 103-minute videocassette is a release of the 1983 motion picture based on the novel by Farley. The VHS is rated PG.

Kerswell, James. *The Complete Book of Horses.* Crescent, 1993. James Kerswell explores all aspects of the world of horses and provides practical information on the selection and care of a horse.

Patent, Dorothy Hinshaw. *Arabian Horses.* Holiday House, 1982. *Arabian Horses* describes the characteristics of the Arabian horse which is known for its speed, beauty, and endurance.

5

Bunnicula
A Rabbit-Tale of Mystery
Deborah and James Howe • Avon, 1979
Reading Level: 6.0 • 112 pages

Summary

Harold, a big Russian Wolfhound, tells the story of Bunnicula from his point of view. Harold's human family discovers a baby rabbit when the family goes to see the movie *Dracula.* The family brings baby Bunnicula home. Harold and another family pet, Chester the cat, hear suspicious noises in the middle of the night and discover white vegetables in the refrigerator. As time goes on, the family pets are convinced that Bunnicula is a vampire bunny.

Website Activities

1. Seaworld

www.seaworld.org/animal_bytes/vampire_batab. html

Busch Gardens Education Department designed this site to provide information on unique creatures in the world. This particular file includes facts about vampire bats.

Activities

 Draw a vampire bat in its natural habitat and include pictures of the animals which would be part of the vampire bat's diet. **[Art]**

Harold and Chester believed that Bunnicula was a vampire bunny because they kept finding white vegetables around the house. Read the information provided on vampire bats. Find at least two similarities Harold discovered between Bunnicula and a vampire bat. Tell one new fact you learned about vampire bats. **[Science]**

Super Search: Why do vampire bats have fewer teeth than other bats?

2. Borzoi (Russian Wolfhound) Club of America

www.thebook.com/borzoi-club-amer/borfaq.htm

This is the official website of The Borzoi (Russian Wolfhound) Club of America. The club promotes the preservation and welfare of the pure bred Borzoi.

Activities

Harold is a Russian Wolfhound. Read the frequently asked questions and answers (FAQ) about Russian Wolfhounds. Tell why this breed of dog would or would not be a good pet for your family. **[Science]**

Select the Borzoi "Photo of the Week" and write your own humorous caption for the photo. **[Language Arts]**

Select "Borzoi Standard." This section describes the characteristics of a Borzoi. Draw a picture of a Borzoi and be sure to include the characteristics described in the article.**[Art]**

Super Search: Can a Russian Wolfhound become friendly with a family cat, like Harold was with Chester?

3. Carpatho-Rusyn Society

www.carpatho-rusyn.org/crs/xmas2.htm

The Carpatho-Rusyn Society is a nonprofit cultural and social organization. Their website is a source of legends, resources, and other items of interest on the Carpatho-Rusyn culture.

Activity

Harold was able to decipher the note found on Bunnicula because the dog was born in Russia and recognized the Carpathian dialect. Read about the Christmas customs celebrated in the

Carpathian Mountain regions and list the customs you would enjoy celebrating. **[Social Studies]**

Super Search: What does a star with a candle signify if it is placed in a window on Christmas Eve?

4. Halloween Magazine

www.halloweenmagazine.com/

Las Vegas, San Jose, and other law and safety enforcement agencies provided information to help develop this site. The site has received numerous awards for "Best Web Page" and for being a "Safe Surf" site.

Activities

Play the Official Halloween Safety Game and learn how to make good decisions when you go trick-or-treating. If you make good choices, you will be presented with a personal award. **[Health]**

Select "Halloween Activities" and then "Halloween Decorations." Read the poem and the directions for making the poem come alive by using props and sound effects. Write your own scary Halloween poem and have your classmates help you perform it. Use special effects in your performance. **[Language Arts]**

Super Search: How many days will it be until Halloween?

5. Nutrition Book Hunt

www.carolhurst.com/subjects/nutritionhunt.html

Carol Hurst's Children's Literature site is a collection of reviews of great books, ideas on ways to use them in the classroom, and activities for curriculum areas and themes.

The veterinarian diagnosed Bunnicula's problem as being malnutrition. Play the "Nutrition Book Hunt" at this site. You may use your school library, local library, or the Internet to locate book titles and authors to complete the activity. You may not use any of the answers given as examples. **[Health]**

Super Search: Which book written by James Howe was given as a sample answer in this activity?

On Your Own

Dracula, Russian Wolfhounds, rabbits, veterinarians, Carpathian Mountains, dialects, Halloween, garlic, vampire bats, vitamin deficiencies

Suggested Reading

Howe, James. *The Celery Stalks at Midnight*. Macmillan, 1983. Harold the dog, and Chester the cat, are still convinced that Bunnicula is a vampire bunny—especially when both pets find a collection of white vegetables.

———. *Howliday Inn*. Hearst, 1982. Chester and Harold spend their summer vacation at a kennel run by a mad scientist.

———. *Nighty-Nightmare*. Atheneum, 1987. The Monroe family pets go on an overnight camping trip and hear the story of how Bunnicula was born.

Additional Sources

Bunnicula. Worldvision Home Video, 1977. This 23 minute videocassette is based on the book *Bunnicula*.

McRae, Gail C. *Borzois*. TFH Publications, 1990. Gail McRae provides information on the selection, feeding, training, health care, and grooming of the Russian Wolfhound.

Retan, Walter. *Bunnies, Bunnies*. Simon & Schuster Books for Young Readers, 1992. Walter Retan compiled this collection of stories, poems, and songs about bunnies.

Wellington, Monica. *Night Rabbits*. Dutton Children's Books, 1995. *Night Rabbits* is a children's book which depicts the nighttime activities of young rabbits in text and illustration.

The Cat Ate My Gymsuit
Paula Danziger • Dell, 1974
Reading Level: 5.5 • 154 pages

Summary

Marcy is thrilled when Ms. Finney becomes her English teacher and challenges her to excel in ways she had never imagined—both academically and personally. However, the controversial teaching methods Ms. Finney uses get her in trouble with the principal and the school board. Marcy and her friends rally to support the suspended teacher with a student protest. These actions lead to consequences that Marcy must face.

Website Activities

1. Food Guide Pyramid

www.nal.usda.gov:8001/py/pmap.htm

The Food and Nutrition Information Center is one of several information centers at the National Agricultural Library. The Center's website includes information on nutrition and food safety.

Activity

Marcy tried to eat nutritious foods so she could lose weight. The Food Guide Pyramid is an outline of what you should eat each day—based on dietary guidelines. Study the food guide pyramid and read the information about each individual section of the pyramid. Make your own pyramid and decorate the six sections of the pyramid with food pictures similar to the pyramid at this Web page. Tomorrow, color a section of the pyramid each time you are finished eating the number of servings required for that particular food group. If you eat a healthy diet, your pyramid should be completely colored by the end of the day. Do not eat more servings than the number required or you will consume too many calories.**[Health]**

Super Search: Which group requires the most servings?

2. Fast Food Facts

www.olen.com/food

The information at this site is derived from the handbook *Fast Food Facts* published by the Consumer Division of the Minnesota Attorney General's Office.

Activities

Eating healthy is difficult when you go to fast food restaurants. Use the "Food Finder" to help you make intelligent choices when you eat at restaurants. Select a fast food restaurant where you eat often. Write down the items you eat for a typical meal in the restaurant. Copy the number of calories, fat grams, percentage of calories from fat, maximum grams of sodium, and milligrams of cholesterol for each item on your meal. Total the numbers in each category. Follow the same procedure for two other fast food restaurants and total the numbers for a typical meal you would eat there. Based on your results, which of the three meals is the most nutritious? **[Health]**

Order a free "Fast Food Facts" pamphlet by e-mailing the address at this site. The pamphlet was prepared by the Minnesota Attorney General's Office. Check with your teacher or parent for permission before you send the e-mail request. **[Language Arts]**

Super Search: How many fast food restaurants are there in the United States?

3. Kids Health

kidshealth.org/parent/behavior/tgr_index97.html

Kids Health is a website devoted to the health of children and teens. It was created by the medical experts at The Nemours Foundation.

Activity

🖱 Stuart's favorite toy was Wolf, his stuffed teddy bear. Visit this website and read the toy and game reviews. Each toy is rated on a "Fun-O-Meter." Use the facts you know about Stuart's personality and character traits to choose a toy you think he would like. Make sure the toy is age-appropriate for Stuart and look carefully at the skills required in order to use the toy. Write your reasons for selecting this toy for Stuart.

[Language Arts]

Super Search: What is the name of the award given to a toy which promotes exceptional learning and good values?

4. Nene Award

www.hcc.hawaii.edu/hspls/nene.html

The Hawaii State Public Library System's Home Page is a "jumping off" point to many informative and entertaining Internet sites in Hawaii and around the world.

Activity

🖱 Paula Danzinger's *The Cat Ate My Gymsuit* was presented the Nene Award in 1980. The award began in 1959 when a group of third graders decided to create a book award. Read the guidelines for the award which was designed by the children. Since then the Nene Award has grown and now over 8,600 children vote for the Nene Award winner. Write your own guidelines for a special book award. Have the students in your classroom nominate books which fit your criteria and allow the students to vote for their favorite book on the list. **[Language Arts]**

Super Search: Which book won the Nene Award for 1998?

5. Fitness File

fyiowa.webpoint.com/fitness/fundhome.htm

This fitness link was created by FYIowa—Iowa's News and Information Network. The Fitness File includes fitness fundamentals and health and fitness information.

Activities

🖱 Marcy never wanted to participate in gym class. Read "Benefits of an Active Lifestyle" on this Web page and then "Take the Fitness Quiz" to test your fitness knowledge.**[Health]**

Super Search: How often do you need to exercise to improve your heart health?

On Your Own

fat, diet, nutrition, communication skills, group dynamics, gym class, women's liberation, children of divorced parents, underage drinking, Weight Watchers, ACLU, bibliotherapy

Suggested Reading

Danziger, Paula. *There's a Bat in Bunk Five*. Delacorte, 1980. Marcy is now fourteen years old and she tries to cope with being on her own when she works as a counselor at an arts camp.

Additional Sources

The Cat Ate My Gymsuit. Baker and Taylor Video, 1995. This videotape in VHS format is based on Paula Danziger's book *The Cat Ate My Gymsuit*.

Schwarzenegger, Arnold. *Fitness for Kids Ages 11–14*. Doubleday, 1993. *Fitness for Kids* is a guide to health, exercise, and nutrition for children 11–14.

7

Catherine, Called Birdy
Karen Cushman • HarperCollins, 1994
Reading Level: 7.4 • 212 pages

Summary

Catherine, a young girl living during the Middle Ages, is disgusted with the inequities she faces. She records her frustrations in a daily journal, talks to her songbirds, and paints murals on her bedroom walls. She is determined to keep her father from arranging an unwanted marriage.

Website Activities

1. Middle Ages Think Quest

tqjunior.advanced.org/4051/instrg.htm

A team of fourth graders from Sanford Hills Elementary School in Harleysville, Pennsylvania, constructed this site on the Middle Ages as an entry in the Think Quest Junior Contest—a national contest recognizing exemplary computer programs designed by students.

Activities

Play the "Castle Game" and learn about objects you would find in a medieval castle. If you answer the questions correctly, King Zealamen will be pleased with your efforts and you will be knighted. **[Social Studies]**

Select "Information" and read the facts given for each of the featured topics for "Life in the Middle Ages." Use the information you learned from reading *Catherine, Called Birdy*, to write one of your own topics. List facts and explain your topic in detail. You may write your own topic or choose from one of the following: weddings, herbal remedies, saints, soap-making, women's roles in the Middle Ages, family life.
[Social Studies, Language Arts]

Super Search: What is the name of the largest room in the castle?

2. Hot Spot for Birds

www.multiscope.com/hotspot/care1.htm

Hot Spot for Birds is a family-friendly avian reference center with informative articles intended to help keep your bird safe and healthy.

Activity

Catherine received great pleasure from raising her songbirds. Visit the Hot Spot for Birds and read the "Bird Care Guide." Based on the information in the guide, write a few paragraphs describing whether or not you feel you would make a good pet bird owner. **[Science, Language Arts]**

Super Search: What is the name for a bird doctor?

3. Literacy Volunteers of America

literacyvolunteers.org/about/

This site is maintained by The Literacy Volunteers of America, a national nonprofit educational organization which delivers tutoring services through a network of volunteers.

Activity

Perkins asked Catherine to teach him to read. Select "FAQs" and read the facts on illiteracy in America. Select "How To's" and learn how you can help solve our nation's illiteracy problems. Write for more information or e-mail the address provided. Check with a teacher or parent before you send your letter or submit your e-mail.
[Language Arts]

Super Search: When was Literacy Volunteers founded?

4. Annenberg/CPBProject

www.learner.org/exhibits/middleages/

This educational site is an Annenberg/CPBProject funded by the Annenberg School of Communications. The Project leads the nation in helping schools and organizations use telecommunication technologies to improve learning.

Activities

Catherine's family lived in a small community during the Middle Ages. Read the facts about what it was really like to live in the Middle Ages. Catherine ministered to the sick and injured by providing herbal remedies to her patients. Select "Health" and try your hand at medieval medicine by diagnosing and trying to cure the cases of three patients at this site. **[Health]**

Select "Arts and Entertainment" and try your luck as a medieval musician. Listen to the sounds of three medieval instruments and try to identify the pictures of the instruments.**[Music]**

Catherine spent much of her time sewing, embroidering, and writing in her diary. In the "Arts and Entertainment" section, choose "Story Weaver" and view a tapestry of medieval life from the Metropolitan Museum of Art in New York City. Write a story about the scene in the tapestry and submit it to the site. You can also read stories that others have written. Be sure to receive permission from your teacher or parent before submitting your story. **[Art, Language Arts]**

Select "clothing" to read about the clothing of medieval royalty, merchants, and monks. Play the "Medieval Hat Game" and determine who would have worn the hats pictured at this site. **[Social Studies]**

Super Search: What was the medieval term for peasants?

5. The Soap Factory

www.alcasoft.com/soapfact/history.html

A small soapmaking company, The Soap Factory, prepared this online booklet to inform people about the history and techniques of soapmaking.

Activity

Making soap was a chore Catherine despised. Read about the history of soapmaking and compare and contrast the methods used by the following groups of people who made soap: The Romans and Celtics, the Northern Europeans, and the American Colonists. **[Social Studies]**

On Your Own

knights, Middle Ages, monks, Scottish castles, songbirds, herbal remedies, ice skating, weddings, dowry, saints, Medieval literature, murals, Vikings, The Crusades

Suggested Reading

Cushman, Karen. *The Ballad of Lucy Whipple.* Clarion, 1996. Lucy is distraught when her mother moves the family cross-country from Massachusetts to a California mining town in 1849.

————. *The Midwife's Apprentice.* Clarion, 1995. A homeless girl in medieval England is raised by a mean-tempered midwife. The young girl learns to deal with great hardships and in the end gains the things she most wants.

Ellis, Anne Leo. *The Dragon of Middlethorpe.* Henry Holt, 1991. Thirteen-year-old Kate is forbidden to join a dragon hunt when the medieval villagers begin their search for the mystical dragon and its treasures.

Additional Sources

Catherine, Called Birdy. Recorded Books, 1996. *Catherine, Called Birdy* is recorded on these five sound cassettes narrated by Jenny Sterlin.

Miguel, Pierre. *The Days of Knights and Castles.* Silver Burdett, 1980. This pictorial history of the Middle Ages from 1066–1485 includes notable events and information on the daily life of people from medieval times.

The Cay
Theodore Taylor • Avon Books, 1969
Reading Level: 6.0 • 144 pages

Summary

Phillip and his mother flee the island of Curacao when their lives are threatened by a German invasion of the area in 1942. Their boat is torpedoed and Phillip becomes stranded on a raft in the ocean with an elderly black man named Timothy. Phillip is blinded and Timothy helps him learn how to survive on a deserted island.

Website Activities

1. National Federation of the Blind

www.nfb.org/kids.htm

The National Federation of the Blind administers this site, which has a wealth of information about blindness.

Activity

Phillip was blind for a period of time and he had to learn how to survive on the island without his eyesight. The National Federation of the Blind provides information about blindness. Read the answers to questions which were asked by children who wanted to know more about how people deal with blindness. Write an essay describing how difficult you think it was for Phillip to cope with blindness, especially since he was on a deserted island. Use the information you learned at this site to support your opinions.
[Language Arts]

Super Search: What is the name of the system which uses raised dots on paper to form letters and words for blind people to read?

2. Ropers' Knot Site

huizen2.dds.nl/~erpprs/kne/kroot.htm

The Ropers' Knot Site has a web knot index and instructions on tying a variety of knots.

Activity

During the hurricane, Timothy tied Phillip and himself to a palm tree. He knotted the rope with a sailor knot. Look at the instruction pages for tying knots at this site. Find two other knots Timothy could have used to serve the same purpose. Follow the directions and diagrams and practice tying some of the knots by using a string or rope.
[Language Arts]

Super Search: What are knots tied at the end of a rope called?

3. Gray's Reef National Marine Sanctuary

www.graysreef.nos.noaa.gov

Gray's Reef National Marine Sanctuary produces this educational site. The sanctuary is located near Sapelo Island in Georgia.

Activity

Find the subheading "Educational Resource." Select "Tales of Whales, Turtles, Sharks, and Snails" and then select "Sharks." Read the information provided about sharks. When you are finished, select "Shark Activities." Print the crossword puzzle and complete it. Print the comparative anatomies of a shark and a bony fish. Fill in the missing data on the diagram. **[Science]**

Super Search: What happens to a shark when it is not swimming?

4. Miami Museum of Science

www.miamisci.org/hurricane/plane.html

The Miami Museum of Science in Miami, Florida, promotes science literacy through this website.

Activities

🖱 Timothy and Phillip lived through a hurricane. They had no one to warn them about the storm. Some airplanes are designed to fly right into the eye of a storm to determine the intensity of the storm. Read about these "hurricane hunters" in this article. Click on the airplane picture and you can make a "weather plane" of your own. **[Science, Art]**

🖱 Read the safety rules for surviving a hurricane. Print the "hurricane shopping list" and make a hurricane survival kit filled with the items on the list. **[Health]**

Super Search: Why is it necessary to store clean water in advance of a hurricane?

5. Martin Luther King

web66.coled.umn.edu/new/MLK/MLK.html

This website is a project of the University of Minnesota's College of Education and Human Development, the Office of Information Technology, and the Center for Applied Research and Educational Improvement.

Activity

🖱 Theodore Taylor's dedication in *The Cay* reads—"To Dr. King's dream, which can only come true if the very young know and understand." Read Martin Luther King, Jr.'s "I Have a Dream" speech which was delivered on August 28, 1963. Write an essay describing your feelings about Theodore Taylor's treatment of racial prejudice in the book. Tell whether you believe Taylor helped to fulfill King's dream by writing the novel. **[Social Studies, Language Arts]**

Super Search: Where did Martin Luther King deliver his famous "I Have a Dream" speech?

On Your Own

Curacao, flying fish, prejudice, Caribbean music, braille, sharks, sea urchins, coconuts, West Indies, sting ray, hurricanes, malaria, moray eel

Suggested Reading

Alexander, Sally Hobart. *Mom Can't See Me.* Macmillan: Collier, 1990. A nine-year-old girl describes how her mother leads an active life despite the fact she is blind.

Stevenson, Robert Louis. *Treasure Island.* Bantam, 1992. A mistress and her son find a treasure map which leads them to a pirate's fortune and an exciting adventure.

Taylor, Theodore. *Timothy of the Cay.* Harcourt Brace, 1993. *Timothy of the Cay* is a prequel-sequel to *The Cay.* Part of the story takes place before Timothy and Phillip are shipwrecked on the island and the other part follows Phillip's life from his rescue to his return to the cay to pay his last respects to Timothy.

Additional Sources

Guide to Caribbean Marine Life. Bennett Marine Video, 1998. This 38-minute videocassette is a documentary describing the miraculous creatures of the Caribbean reefs.

Lessac, Fran e. *Caribbean Alphabet.* Tambourine Books, 1994. An alphabet of pictures is presented with images from the Caribbean.

Weiss, Malcolm E. *Blindness.* Franklin Watts, 1980. This resource explains how those who are afflicted with blindness learn how to overcome it.

Charlotte's Web
E.B. White • Harper and Row, 1952
Reading Level: 6.0 • 184 pages

Summary

Wilbur is the runt in a litter of pigs. He fears he will be slaughtered and turned into bacon. The barnyard animals unite in an effort to keep Wilbur alive. A kind and motherly spider named Charlotte takes him "under her web" and uses her ingenuity to save Wilbur's life.

Website Activities

1. Pork Council

www.nppc.org/foodfun.html

This is the World Wide Website of the National Pork Producers Council. It is a site for pork lovers, pork producers, and anyone who wants to learn more about pigs and pork.

Activities

Select "Kids" and "Around the World with Pork." Take an international adventure through a magical pantry by participating in the interactive story called, "The Kid, the Pork, and the Pantry." **[Language Arts]**

Select "Games Gallery" and solve the nutrition puzzles on the Web page. For an extra challenge, test your nutrition knowledge with the "5 Food Group Pyramid Game." **[Health]**

Super Search: What is the name of the Hawaiian-style roasted pig wrapped in leaves?

2. 4-H

www.4h-usa.org/

This is the official home page for the National 4-H. 4-H is recognized nationally and worldwide as a leader in providing fun learning activities and materials for youth from K–12.

Activity

Currently 47 percent of 4-H members live on farms, in rural areas, or in very small towns. 4-H emphasizes working with vulnerable youth in urban and highly isolated rural communities. Select "Red, White, Blue and Green" and then "Hearts and Hands" to check out the various programs provided across the country by 4-H. Choose a program you feel would be worthwhile and tell how your community would benefit from this program. **[Language Arts]**

Super Search: What do each of the "H's" in 4-H represent?

3. Vocabulary University

www.vocabulary.com/index.html

Vocabulary University is maintained by Corey Orr Cook and his wife Jan. They provide free vocabulary puzzles to enhance vocabulary mastery. The site has been endorsed by teachers because it enriches classroom curriculum and helps to prepare students for the SAT and PSAT exams.

Activity

E.B. White used Charlotte in the story to improve Wilbur's and the readers' vocabulary. Charlotte spoke a word such as "humble" and then explained to Wilbur that "humble" means "not proud." Educate and entertain yourself at this excellent vocabulary building website. Begin playing puzzles at Level 1 and submit your answers. You will get immediate feedback about the number of correct answers you give. You will also be given the use of the words in context. The site provides you with other helpful hints to assist you in improving your vocabulary. If Level 1 seems too easy, you can try Level 2 or 3. When you complete twelve sessions, you will receive a

Vocabulary University Diploma. **[Language Arts]**

Super Search: How many words do you need to learn before you earn your diploma?

4. Entomology and Arachnology

pioneer.mov.vic.gov.au/spiders/games.html

Dr. Ken Walker, Senior Curator of Entomology, is the developer of this site on Entomology and Arachnology at the Museum Victoria in Melbourne, Australia.

Activity

Play the Spider games at this site and learn more about the characteristics of spiders. You will need at least Netscape 3.0 on your computer to play the game "Neurosis." **[Science]**

Super Search: When you play the game "Hangman," which type of letter shouldn't you use?

5. Ferris Wheels

ecss.eng.iastate.edu/explorer/park/fwm.htm

This Web page was created by Janelle Boeding during an internship program at Iowa State University called the Program for Women in Science and Engineering. The site answers many questions on the history of Ferris wheels and how Ferris wheels work.

Activities

The Ferris wheel was the most popular ride at the county fair. Select "Where did the Ferris wheel come from?" Read the article and make a timeline with dates and facts you learned about the Ferris wheel. **[Social Studies]**

Select "Build Your Own Ferris Wheel" from Legos, and you have permission from the creator to print the instructions. **[Art]**

Select "Rides Like the Ferris Wheel." Look at the pictures and the descriptions of the rides. List the rides you have been on and the ones which you would enjoy riding. **[Language Arts]**

Super Search: What was another name for Ferris wheels?

On Your Own

pigs, care of farm animals, spiders, crickets, county fairs, amusement rides, farming, spider webs, near-sightedness, fact/fantasy, increasing vocabulary

Suggested Reading

Herriot, James. *Treasury for Children.* St. Martin's Press, 1992. James Herriot compiled this anthology of his award-winning stories for children.

Peck, Robert Newton, and Jack Hess. *A Day No Pigs Would Die.* Dell, 1972. A thirteen-year-old Vermont farm boy is distraught when his father wants to slaughter the family's pet pig because it cannot produce a litter.

White, E.B. *Stuart Little.* Harper Trophy, 1973. Stuart Little is a mouse who sets out in the world to find his dearest friend, a little bird who stayed with Stuart for a few days in the family's garden.

Additional Sources

Charlotte's Web. Bantam Doubleday Dell, 1991. This the audio CD edition of the original book. The text refers to the hardcover edition of E. B. Whites' *Charlotte's Web.*

Parsons, Alexandra. *Amazing Spiders.* Knopf, 1990. *Amazing Spiders* has text and photographs to introduce the different species of spiders.

10

The Chocolate Touch
Patrick Skene Catling • Bantam Doubleday Dell, 1952
Reading Level: 4.0 • 88 pages

Summary

John's mother is concerned when he only eats chocolate and refuses to eat his vegetables. John eats a unique chocolate candy and he soon discovers that the candy gives him magical powers. At first, John is excited when he can turn ordinary objects into chocolate. However, one day he kisses his mother and gets a big surprise.

Website Activities

1. Carol's Webpage

members.xoom.com/satin1/children.htm

This is a literature-based website which includes over 60 children's stories, virtual cards, and quotable quotes.

Activities

Select "The Midas Touch" and read the story about a king who loved gold. Make a list of the similarities between the two stories: "The Chocolate Touch" and "The Midas Touch." Include the following elements of fiction in your list and tell how the elements are related in both stories: characters, character traits, character goals, plot, problem/solution, setting and theme. **[Language Arts]**

Read several of the other stories on this website. Select one of the legends and make changes to create your own modern-day version. Do this by keeping the plot basically the same but by changing other elements. When your creative story is finished, read it to the class and see if your classmates can tell which story it is based on. **[Language Arts]**

Super Search: In which country did King Midas live?

2. Hershey Foods

www.hersheys.com/kidztown

Hershey Foods Corporation created this website to provide entertainment, information, and education.

Activities

Select "Recipes for Kids." Read the tips for "Safe Cooking in the Kitchen." Use the tips to create a poster which can be used as a reference and hung in your kitchen. Be sure to use the tips whenever you are cooking at home. **[Health, Art]**

Select "Try These Special Recipes." Read the chocolate recipes. Ask a relative or neighbor for a favorite chocolate recipe and bring a copy of the recipe to class. Collect the recipes from each of your classmates and make a classroom chocolate recipe book. **[Language Arts]**

Super Search: Where is Hershey Chocolate's plant located in North America?

3. Kids Candy

www.kidscandy.org/k_health.html

The Kids Candy site is sponsored by the National Confectioners' Association and The Chocolate Manufacturers' Association. Both organizations provide nutritional information about candy.

Activity

John got into trouble when he ignored his health by eating candy. Read the three articles at this site dealing with the facts and myths on candy. Use the information you learn to write a speech you would give to John persuading him to eat a balanced diet and informing him about making healthy nutritional choices. **[Health, Language Arts]**

Super Search: How many milligrams of caffeine are there in an ounce of milk chocolate?

4. Instrument Encyclopedia

www.lehigh.edu/zoellner/encyclopedia.html

This site was created by the Zoellner Arts Center located on the Lehigh University Campus in Bethlehem, Pennsylvania.

Activities

John enjoyed playing the trumpet in his school orchestra. Tour the instruments in the "Instrument Encyclopedia" by reading a description of each instrument and listening to music played by the instruments. Select an instrument you might be interested in learning how to play and tell why you chose that particular instrument. You will need to have "real audio" on your computer to play the music. **[Music]**

Select "Guess the Instrument" and quiz yourself on the names of the instruments listed in the "Instrument Encyclopedia." **[Music]**

Super Search: Which instrument is the largest bowed stringed instrument in the modern orchestra?

5. M&M /Mars

www.m-ms.com/

M&M/Mars created this website for children which includes fun, activities, and information about M&M's Chocolate Candies.

Activities

Select "M&M's Studios" and then "Blue's Poetry Cafe." Read the poems written by the M&Ms. Listen to the poems being performed at the cafe. You will need to use "Real Player" if you want to hear the poetry. Write your own poem for the brown M&M. Perform it for your classmates. **[Language Arts]**

Super Search: In which year did the Spanish colonists bring a chocolate drink to Europe?

On Your Own

The Midas Touch, orchestral instruments, candy, chocolate, balanced diet/nutrition, coin collecting, magic, jumping rope, school lunches, music class, birthday parties

Suggested Reading

Cormier, Robert. *Chocolate War*. Pantheon, 1974. A high school freshman refuses to join in the high school's fundraising drive to sell chocolate candy and has to suffer the consequences of his decision.

Howe, James. *Hot Fudge*. Avon Camelot, 1991. The Monroes leave Harold at home alone with a pan of chocolate fudge.

Smith, Robert. *Chocolate Fever*. Bantam Doubleday Dell, 1972. Henry eats too much chocolate and breaks out in a chocolate rash. He runs away from home and becomes involved with two hijackers who are being chased by the police.

Additional Sources

Dineen, Jacqueline. *Chocolate*. Carolrhoda, 1991. *Chocolate* discusses where chocolate comes from, its history, and how it is processed for eating.

Milton Hershey: The Chocolate King. New Video Group, 1996. This 50 minute videorecording on VHS format is a biography of Milton S. Hershey — the man who started the Hershey Chocolate company.

11

The Cricket in Times Square
George Selden • Dell, 1960
Reading Level: 6.2 • 180 pages

Summary

Chester the Cricket climbs into a picnic basket in Connecticut and wakes up in Grand Central Station in New York City. He is found by a little boy and taken to his new home in a newsstand in Times Square. Chester is befriended by a cat and a mouse and they encourage him to develop his extraordinary talent for singing.

Website Activities

1. Times Square
63.67.194.190/

The Times Square Business Improvement District was established to make Times Square clean, safe, and friendly. The organization provides this site as a promotion for the area.

Activity

Chester Cricket went back to Connecticut before he had the opportunity to visit New York City's Times Square on New Year's Eve. Select "Events" and then "New Year's Eve in Times Square." Use the information you learned from the story and this website to write five things Chester would have seen if he were in Times Square on New Year's Eve. **[Language Arts]**

Super Search: What was the year of the first Ball Lowering celebration in Times Square?

2. Songs of Crickets and Katydids from Japan
www.asahi-net.or.jp/~UN6K-HSMT/English/ENGindex.htm

This is a Japanese site created by Kazuyuki Hasimoto.

Activity

Chester Cricket charmed the people in New York City with his beautiful songs. Select "Crickets and Katydids" and listen to the actual cricket sounds from seventeen different kinds of crickets. Choose the cricket at this site that looks most like the cricket in the story. You will need "Real Player" loaded on your computer in order to listen to the cricket songs. **[Science]**

Super Search: Which cricket picture resembles a grasshopper?

3. Cricket Magazine
www.cricketmag.com/cricket/index.html

This is the official home page of "Cricket Magazine." The magazine updates this online version each month.

Activities

Join Chester Cricket's family at "Cricket Magazine" and visit "Mimi's Library." Select "Recommended Reading" and read the recommendations made by other magazine readers. If you enjoyed reading *The Cricket in Times Square*, write your own critic's review and post it at this site. You may post a review for a different children's book if you prefer. Please show your recommendation to your teacher, librarian, or parent before you actually post it to the Internet. **[Language Arts]**

Select "Cricket League" and read the instructions for entering this month's contest. After you receive permission from an adult, send in your entry and the prize winning entries will be published by "Cricket Magazine." **[Language Arts]**

Super Search: What is the name of the publishing company holding the copyright license for this site?

4. The New York Times

nytimes.com

This is the official Internet version of the New York Times newspaper. The site is constantly being updated to provide readers with the most current news.

Activity

Mr. Smedly wrote a letter to the music editor of the *New York Times* to inform the people of New York about a musical miracle—the cricket. Check out the online version of the *New York Times*. In the "New York Today" section, select "music" in the "find favorite" box. This Web page will give you the locations for all types of musical concerts and shows in New York City. Mr. Smedly would have enjoyed attending an opera. Select "classical/opera" and see how many operas will be presented today in the New York City area. **[Music]**

Super Search: What is the present temperature in New York City?

5. The Book of Gods, Goddesses, Heroes, and Other Characters of Mythology

www.cybercomm.net/~grandpa/grkgdsnp.html

This website was created by P.J. Criss. This particular section of the site introduces Greek Mythological characters.

Activities

Mario's music teacher told the story of Orpheus, the greatest musician who ever lived. Find the character description of "Orpheus" and list ways that Chester Cricket was like Orpheus. **[Language Arts]**

Select one of the other mythological characters featured on this website. Draw a picture of the character by using the character traits provided in the description. Collect the pictures done by your classmates and arrange them to create a Mythology Mural for your classroom. **[Art]**

Super Search: What was the name of Orpheus's wife?

On Your Own

mouse, Times Square, subways, Grand Central Station, New York City, crickets, New Year's Eve, Orpheus, Chinatown, Chinese food, Chinese customs, jobs for kids, opera

Suggested Reading

Holman, Felice. *The Cricket in Winter.* Dell, 1974. Sylvester discovers he can communicate with a cricket who lives under the floorboards in his bedroom.

Leonard, Marcia. *Crickets: Jokes, Riddles, and Other Stuff.* Random House, 1977. Marcia Leonard's book is a compilation of cricket cartoons, jokes, and riddles.

Selden, George. *Chester Cricket's New Home.* Farrar Straus & Giroux, 1983. Chester the Cricket has to search for a new home when two hefty ladies sit on his stump and it collapses.

Additional Sources

The Cricket in Times Square. BDD Audio Publishing, 1995. This is a double-sided audiocassette version of *The Cricket in Times Square.*

Johnson, Sylvia A. *Chirping Insects.* Lerner, 1986. This Lerner National Science Book describes how chirping insects produce their songs and use them to send messages to their fellow critters.

Plotkin, Fred, and Placido Domingo. *Opera 101: A Complete Guide to Learning and Loving the Opera.* Hyperion, 1994. Placido Domingo is featured in this book which is a guide to learning about opera appreciation.

12 Dragonwings

Laurence Yep • HarperCollins, 1975
Reading Level: 6.6 • 248 pages

Summary

Moon Shadow's father lives in San Francisco and works in a laundry shop trying to save enough money to send for his wife and son in China. When Moon Shadow turns eight years old, he sails from China to join his father. Father is obsessed with thoughts of flying and he engages Moon Shadow in his dream of building an airplane. The two Chinese-Americans have a difficult time dealing with the demons (white Americans) and with the ridicule they receive from their Chinese countrymen for following their dream.

Website Activities

1. Karate One

www.karate1.com/

This is the home page of Karate One. The site is filled with facts about martial arts and karate. Clip art for the Chinese alphabet is also provided.

Activity

When Moon Shadow's mother wrote letters to him, the letters were written in Chinese characters instead of in the letters of the English alphabet. Select "Alphabet" and view the Chinese characters for letters, numbers, and punctuation marks. Writing Chinese characters takes a great deal of practice. Have each student in your class select a different character of the Chinese alphabet. Each student should copy the character on a piece of construction paper and the letters can be hung on the wall near the English alphabet. **[Language Arts]**

Super Search: Which Chinese character is the same for both the upper case and lower case letter?

2. First Flight

firstflight.open.ac.uk/

This site is part of a project concerned with the development of virtual science environments over the web. It was developed by Multimedia Enabling Technologies Group, Knowledge Media Institute, and the United Kingdom's Open University.

Activity

Windrider was inspired by the Wright Brothers and their successful flight at Kitty Hawk. Select "Frederick Hooven's simulation" and experience the following:

1. View a movie of the first flight as seen from Orville's eyes.

2. Receive flight instructions and fly a flight simulator.

3. View a movie of a flight Wilbur made in Italy.

You will need to have Shockwave loaded on your computer to fly the simulator. **[Science]**

Super Search: What was the date of Orville Wright's first controlled, powered, flight?

3. Eye Witness

www.ibiscom.com/sfeq.htm

Eye Witness is a site which recounts history through the words of those who were there. It uses personal stories and other first-hand sources to tell about the past and to bring history to life.

Activity

The story of the San Francisco Earthquake of 1906 was told from Moon Shadow's point of view. Read these accounts of the Earthquake told by eye witnesses to the same disaster. Describe the earthquake from Windrider's point of view. Tell about what he experienced and how you think he felt during the devastating earthquake. **[Social Studies]**

Super Search: How many people were killed during the earthquake of 1906?

4. The Abacus

http://www.ee.ryerson.ca:8080/~elf/abacus

Created by Luis Fernandes. This site provides information on the art of calculating with beads. The site has won numerous Web awards and has been featured in several publications.

Activity

Moon Shadow learned how to calculate with an abacus when he lived in China. Read the instructions on how to use an abacus. Write a few paragraphs telling whether you would rather use a calculator or an abacus to do your homework. **[Math]**

Super Search: Which civilization was the first to use the abacus?

5. The Dome of the Sky

einstein.stcloudstate.edu/Dome/clicks/constlist.html

The Dome of the Sky is an Online Planetarium which allows you to view the stars and learn the names of the stars and constellations. A brief mythology is given for each constellation. The site is sponsored by St.Cloud State University in St. Cloud, Minnesota.

Activity

Father told stories to Moon Shadow and Robin about the stars in the constellations. Most of the 88 constellations are associated with Roman and Greek myths. A myth is a traditional story which usually includes deeds of gods or heroes and it explains something which occurs in nature. Read these myths based on the constellations. The constellation Camelopardus has no classical myth associated with it. Write your own myth describing Camelopardus. Be sure to include a god, goddess, or hero and explain why the constellation is called The Giraffe. **[Language Arts]**

Super Search: How many constellations are there in the south polar region of the sky?

6. Big Sky Records

www.bigskymusic.com/b-world.htm

Big Sky Records is a production company that was created to bring together music and art from different cultures. The company distributes its products through Warner Music.

Activity

View the pictures of Chinese musical instruments and read the descriptions for each instrument. Tell which instruments from your own experience would be similar to the Chinese featured on this site. Click on "Releases" to hear recordings of Chinese music. **[Music]**

Super Search: Which Chinese stringed instrument resembles the Spanish guitar?

On Your Own

Chinese customs, kites, Chinatown, Chinese alphabet, San Francisco cable cars, Chinese calendar, Wright Brothers, dirigibles, abacuses, stereopticons, dragons, hang gliding, constellations, earthquakes

Suggested Reading

Yep, Laurence. *The Case of the Goblin Pearls.* HarperCollins, 1997. A Chinese American actress and her niece try to solve the case of a theft of priceless pearls in San Francisco's Chinatown.

————. *The City of Dragons.* Scholastic, 1995. Nobody wants to look at the sad face of a little boy so he runs away to the City of Dragons where he seeks acceptance.

Additional Sources

Caldecott, Barrie. *Kites.* Franklin Watts, 1990. Kite designs are introduced by text and photographs and information is given for the best material to use in the construction of kites.

Great San Francisco *Earthquake: 1906: American Experience.* Time Life Custom Publishing, 1996. The story of the San Francisco Earthquake is told in the VHS taped edition.

Wright Brothers at Kitty Hawk, This Is America. CB, 1994. This VHS tape tells the story of the Wright Brothers and their historic first flight.

13

Flat Stanley

Jeff Brown • Harper Trophy, 1964
Reading Level: 4.0 • 64 pages

Summary

A bulletin board falls on Stanley and flattens him. Stanley and his family are distressed until they realize there are advantages to being flat. Stanley can fly like a kite, travel to California in an envelope, and assist the Chief of Police in capturing a criminal. Stanley may be flat, but he manages to become a hero.

Website Activities

1. Flat Stanley Project

www.enoreo.on.ca/flatstanley/

The "Flat Stanley Project" is an international literacy and communications activity on the Internet for primary and intermediate students. The project was designed for students who have read *Flat Stanley*.

Activity

Read the information at this site and find out how your class can participate in the Flat Stanley Project. The list of participants is constantly being updated. You can send a Stanley from your classroom to other schools and see what the world is like through Stanley's eyes. **[Language Arts, Social Studies]**

Super Search: If you want to participate in this project, which two items do you need to send through the mail?

2. The Cook's Thesaurus

www.northcoast.com/~alden/

Lori Alden used recipe books, cooking guides, and nutritional research to design this site that suggests substitutions for thousands of cooking ingredients. The site includes low-calorie and low-fat alternatives for dieters, inexpensive substitutes for gourmet cooks on a tight budget, and innovative replacements for hard-to-find ethnic ingredients.

Activity

Mrs. Lambchop made a flat egg salad sandwich for Stanley to take with him when he was mailed in an envelope to California. Use this website to make a list of other flat foods which Stanley would enjoy. **[Health]**

Super Search: Name a vegetable that would be considered a tuber.

3. U.S. Post Office

www.usps.gov/postofc/welcome.htm

This post office is open seven days a week, 24 hours a day because it is a website written and produced by the United States Post Office.

Activities

Use the "Postage Calculator" from the side bar list to determine how much it would cost you to send Flat Stanley from your hometown to California. Follow these directions:

1. Select "Large envelope."

2. Enter your zip code.

3. Type the zip code for Los Angeles, California: 90001.

4. Select "US postage rates."

5. Type: 2 pounds 0 ounces.

Tell how much it would cost to mail the envelope parcel post, priority mail, and express mail.

The US Postal Service releases new stamps every year. Select "Stamps" and "Directory of Stamp Images" to view pictures of the latest stamps. Take a poll in your class to see which stamp is the most popular. **[Social Studies]**

Super Search: What is the 1-800 number you should use if you want to buy postage stamps?

4. Lincoln Electric Systems

www.les.lincoln.ne.us/kids/kite2.htm#top

Lincoln Electric Systems in Lincoln, Nebraska, designed this site to emphasize kite flying safety.

Activities

Select "Print and Play" to print coloring pages about kite safety. Print the mazes, crossword puzzles, and word searches to learn more information on safety. **[Health]**

Take the "Online Quiz" and an Electric Safety Expert will score your answers for you. You can compare your score with the scores of other children who have taken the quiz on the Internet.

Super Search: Name the part of the kite where you attach the string.

5. National Gallery of Art

www.nga.gov/collection/collect.htm

This is the official home page for the National Gallery of Art in Washington, DC.

Activities

Stanley helped the Chief of Police by posing as an art object in the art museum. Take a virtual field trip to the National Gallery of Art. There are more then 100,000 objects in this art collection for you to view. Select your favorite painting or sculpture and tell why you chose this particular one. **[Art]**

Stanley became a hero when he helped capture the art museum thief. Sketch a floor plan of your own art museum. Show where you would station the security guards in your museum by marking each area with an "X." **[Social Studies, Art]**

Super Search: How many different foreign language guides are provided at this site?

6. Map Quest

www.mapquest.com/

Map Quest is an interactive map service which provides maps and driving directions to locations throughout the world.

Activity

Flat Stanley traveled across the United States to California. Select "Driving Directions" and follow these directions:

1. Enter your home address for your starting address.

2. Enter Los Angeles, California for your destination address.

3. Select "City to City."

4. Select "Overview Map with Text."

5. Select "Calculate Directions."

Tell how many miles it is from your home to Los Angeles. **[Social Studies, Math]**

Super Search: How many different roads will you need to travel on to get to Los Angeles?

On Your Own

kites, good manners, California, air travel, US Postal Service, art museums, flat things, travel guides, security guards

Suggested Reading

Brown, Jeff. *Invisible Stanley.* Harper Trophy, 1996. Stanley's family cannot find him when he becomes invisible during a thunderstorm.

Grant, Gwen. *Matthew and His Magic Kite.* Rourke, 1982. Matthew's magic kite enables him to make a special trip to the North Pole.

Additional Sources

Baker, Rhoda. *Making Kites.* Chartwell Books, 1993. *Making Kites* tells how to build and fly your own kites from simple sleds to complex stunters.

National Museum of American Art: Smithsonian Institution. Macmillan Digital USA, 1996. This interactive multimedia production is a computer optical disc. It includes more than 750 major works of art, biographical information on famous artists, and two hours of video, slide presentations, and audio clips.

14

The Great Brain
John D. Fitzgerald • Dell, 1967
Reading Level: 5.0 • 192 pages

Summary

Tom is known in his town as the "Great Brain." He is only ten years old and he has a special knack for solving problems. His younger brother admires him but is also a little perturbed at his brother for some of his actions. Tom always manages to swindle innocent people until the end of the story when something comes over him and he feels "warm and Christmassy."

Website Activities

1. Gamekids

www.gamekids.com/index1.html

This is a gathering place on the Internet for kids of all ages to learn and exchange non-computer games and activities. The site is a joint media project of Media Bridge GameKids and Communication Graphics.

Activities

 Children did not have computers and televisions in the 1800s so they created games to entertain themselves. Some of the games played in *The Great Brain* include hopscotch, marbles, and kick the can. Select "Games" and read the new games and world games submitted to this site by other children. Choose a different game for each day of the week to play with your classmates during recess or after school. At the end of the week, take a survey to determine which game was most-liked by your friends. **[Social Studies]**

 Create your own game. Write the following information on paper:

1. Name of the game
2. Rules of the games
3. Equipment needed

Practice playing your new game with some of your classmates. If it is necessary, make changes in the rules to improve the way the game is played. **[Language Arts]**

 Select "Send a Gamekids Greeting Card" and e-mail one of your friends or classmates a special message. Be sure to receive permission from an adult before you send the card. **[Language Arts]**

Super Search: Name one of the many awards this site has been given.

2. Ben and Jerry's

www.benjerry.com/

Ben and Jerry's Company is known for their specialty ice creams. This site provides ice cream information, games, and arts and crafts.

Activities

 The boys helped Mama make homemade ice cream in the story. Visit the Ben and Jerry's website and select "Fun Stuff" and then "Games." Play the ice cream games at this site. Some of the games require the use of Shockwave or Java. **[Language Arts, Art]**

 Select "Arts and Crafts." You will need paper, scissors, glue, and a printer. Follow the directions given to complete your project. Ben and Jerry's grants you permission to copy the paper crafts, but you should also get permission from your teacher before you use the printer. **[Art]**

 There are many flavors of ice cream. Write the name of your favorite flavor and then create your own original flavor. List the names of the ingredients needed for your special ice cream. **[Language Arts]**

Super Search: Where is the Ben and Jerry Company located?

3. The Math Forum

forum.swarthmore.edu/elempow/

The Math Forum is an online math educational community center funded by the National Science Foundation. The site presents a "Problem of the Week" for both elementary and middle school students.

Activity

Tom was a brain at solving problems. Solve the problem of the week and submit your answer. If you solve the problem correctly, your name will appear on this website and you may be awarded a prize. **[Math]**

Super Search: Which day of the week is the deadline for submitting an answer for the problem of the week?

4. One-Room School Homepage

www.msc.cornell.edu/~weeds/SchoolPages/ welcome.html

This site was written by Bill Wedemeyer, a student at Cornell University. The site contains the accounts of an actual one-room school teacher.

Activities

The children in Adenville attended a one-room schoolhouse. Scroll down the Web page until you locate the link to "a typical school day." Click on the link and read the letters written by a one-room school teacher. List five ways your school day is different from a typical school day in a one-room schoolhouse. **[Language Arts]**

Fold an 8½" x 11" paper in half lengthwise. On one side of the paper, list the advantages of attending a one-room schoolhouse. On the other side, list the disadvantages. Count the number of entries on each side and share you results with the class. **[Language Arts]**

Super Search: When were blackboards introduced to classrooms?

On Your Own

Utah, Mormons, inventions, one-room schoolhouses, cave exploring, problem solving, ice cream, immigrants, malnutrition, gangrene, prosthesis, physical therapy

Suggested Reading

Fitzgerald, John D. *The Great Brain Is Back.* Dial Books for Young Readers, 1995. Tom is still a brain and he loves money but he has matured and he also loves a pretty thirteen-year-old girl.

————. *Me and My Little Brain.* Dial Books for Young Readers, 1971. The Great Brains little brother, J.D., finds he can also accomplish feats with his own little brain.

————. *More Adventures of the Great Brain.* Dial Press, 1969. The Great Brain of Adenville, Utah, continues to be more mischievous with his practical jokes and get-rich-quick schemes.

Additional Sources

Hill, William E. *The Mormon Trail: Yesterday and Today.* Utah State University Press, 1996. William Hill chronicles the lives of Mormons from the past until the present.

Jacobson, Don, and Lee Stral. *Caves and Caving: A Handbook and Guide to American Caves from Simply Enjoying Them to Professional Spelunking.* Harbor House, 1987. This is a handbook and guide on American caves and the exploration of caves.

15

The Great Gilly Hopkins
Katherine Paterson • HarperCollins, 1978
Reading Level: 6.1 • 148 pages

Summary

An angry little girl is forced to move to yet another foster home. Gilly is determined to hate her new foster mother. Despite her bitterness, Gilly learns to find love and acceptance in her new home. When her grandmother shows up and demands that Gilly live with her, Gilly has to start all over in a new home again.

Website Activities

1. Women's National Basketball Association

www.wnba.com

This site is devoted to promoting women's professional basketball and providing the latest statistics and standings for the sport.

Activity

 Gilly enjoyed playing basketball on the playground. Visit the official site of the Women's National Basketball Association. Select "Players" and read a few of the player profiles. Assume that Gilly is old enough to play in the WNBA. Write a player profile for Gilly. Make the profile seem authentic by including facts you know about Gilly's character traits and goals. **[Language Arts, Health]**

Super Search: How many teams are currently in the WNBA?

2. Honeysuckle White

www.honeysucklewhite.com/index.html

This is the official home page of Honeysuckle White. The company is one of the largest turkey processors in the United States.

Activities

 There was no Thanksgiving turkey for Gilly because everyone in the house was sick and Gilly had to take care of them. Select "Just for Fun" and read the fanciful tale of "Lonesome Turkey." Read all eight episodes and write a summary of the story. Include the following information in your summary:

1. Who were the main characters?

2. What was the problem in the story?

3. What major events happened in the story?

4. How was the problem solved?
   [Language Arts]

 Select "Over 100 Great Turkey Recipes" and read several of the turkey recipes. Create your own school lunch. Your meal must include turkey. Tell what other items you would include in the meal to make it nutritious for the students. **[Health]**

Super Search: How many turkeys needed to be taken on the trail drive to the market?

3. Katherine Paterson Site

www.terabithia.com/

Katherine Paterson developed her own personal website. She provides summaries for every book she has written.

Activities

 In April 1998, *The Great Gilly Hopkins* was performed at the New Victory Theater. Read the *New York Times* review of the show and select "streaming audio" to hear an audio clip of Gilly singing in the show. Describe an event from the book that you think would be fun to watch in a musical production of the story. **[Music]**

Select "Frequently Asked Questions" and click on the questions to see Katherine Paterson's answers given during a recent interview with the author. Write three interesting facts you learned about Katherine Paterson. **[Language Arts]**

Super Search: Who directed the musical *The Great Gilly Hopkins?*

4. National Foster Parent Association

www.kidsource.com/nfpa/want.to.be.foster.html

This is the official site for the National Foster Parent Association. NFPA is a nonprofit, volunteer organization established to give support to foster parents across the country.

Activity

Read this article written by Greg Olson, a foster care provider. Make a list of the similarities between Mrs. Trotter's and Mr. Olson's lives. Tell how you think their lives were affected when they decided to become foster parents. **[Language Arts]**

Super Search: When was the NFPA established?

5. Lunaland Online

www.lunaland.co.za/

Lunaland Online is a fun website for kids with interactive stories, puzzles, games, crafts, songs, and wacky news.

Activities

Gilly listened to William Ernest read when he wasn't busy watching Sesame Street. Ask your teacher for permission to have a kindergarten or first grade student visit your class for this activity. Select one of the interactive stories at this site and read it to the younger student. Allow your student to change the names of the characters in the story. Print the story and have the child color it to make his or her own storybook. **[Language Arts]**

Select "Luna Fun" and choose another activity to do with your student. You may choose a game, puzzle, craft, or storybook. **[Language Arts]**

Super Search: What is the name of Katie's pony?

On Your Own

foster parents, Tolkien, WNBA, English verse, William Wordsworth, mental retardation, Sesame Street, prejudice, self-defense, Thanksgiving, social workers

Suggested Reading

Byars, Betsy. *The Pinballs.* Harper and Row, 1977. Three children come to live at a foster home when they can no longer be cared for at their own homes. Their friendship grows as the foster parents nurture them.

Paterson, Katherine. *Bridge to Terabithia.* Crowell, 1977. Jesse becomes best friends with a new neighbor, and they are happy in their special hideaway until Leslie dies trying to reach "Terabithia" during a thunderstorm.

————. *Jacob Have I Loved.* Avon, 1980. Louise tells this story about the jealousy she feels toward her talented and beautiful twin sister.

Thesman, Jean. *When the Road Ends.* Avon Books, 1993. Three foster children and an old woman recovering from an accident are abandoned and forced to survive on their own.

Additional Sources

The Great Gilly Hopkins. Rhache, 1990. This is the video version on VHS format for the story *The Great Gilly Hopkins.*

Johnston, Marianne. *Dealing with Anger.* Power Kids Press, 1996. *Dealing with Anger* suggests ways to deal with anger directly, channel it to something productive, and avoid its destructiveness.

16

Hatchet
Gary Paulsen • Viking Penguin, 1997
Reading Level: 5.5 • 195 pages

Summary

Brian's parents are divorced and his father wants him to fly to the Canadian Northwest to spend the summer with him. While in the air, the pilot suffers a heart attack and dies. Brian is forced to land the plane in a lake in the Canadian wilderness. He is left to survive alone with just his basic instincts and a hatchet.

Website Activities

1. Canada Online

canadaonline.miningco.com/msub11.htm

The Mining Company is a network of comprehensive websites for over 500 topics. The company created net links relating to important Canadian natural resources and environmental issues.

Activities

Brian had encounters in the Canadian wilderness with a moose, a wolf, and a porcupine. Check out the "Wildlife" section at this site and select "Hinterland Who's Who." Look at the index of other Canadian birds and mammals. Use the information you learn about a specific bird or animal to write a few paragraphs on how Brian's adventure would have been different if he had encountered this animal in Canada. **[Science, Language Arts]**

Select "Kid's Treehouse" in the "Student" section. Identify one of the suggestions you could actually use to help protect wildlife in your community. Write a plan for how you would follow through with this suggestion. **[Science, Language Arts]**

Super Search: Name an endangered animal living in Canada.

2. CyberAir Park

www.cyberair.com/audio/chiapp/index.html

CyberAir Park is a group of aviation enthusiasts who promote aviation, safety, and public awareness at this site.

Activity

If Brian had been able to establish radio contact, his plane might not have crashed. Listen to live transmissions from the Chicago O'Hare Airport. You will need to have "Real Audio" loaded on your computer in order to hear the transmissions. **[Science]**

Super Search: Name two other airports located in the same quadrant as O'Hare.

3. CyberAir Park/ FAA publications

www.cyberair.com/tower/faa/pilot/index.html

The United States Department of Transportation Federal Aviation Administration provides two publications with information on obtaining a pilot's license.

Activities

Brian had to fly the plane alone when the pilot died. Select "A Flying Start." Read the requirements for obtaining a pilot's license. Based on this information, tell whether you would be able to meet all of the requirements and obtain a license at your age. **[Language Arts]**

Select "Student Pilot Guide." Send for a student guide and share the information with your class. **[Language Arts]**

Super Search: What is the international language of aviation?

4. The Tech

the-tech.mit.edu/V115/N27/pilot.27w.html

The Tech is an online newspaper published by the Massachusetts Institute of Technology. This article is in the archives of *The Tech* and was written by Dana Priest. It first appeared in the *Washington Post*, Vol. 115, #27 on June 9, 1995.

Activities

Captain Scott F. O'Grady was a downed Air Force pilot who survived in Bosnia for six days by recalling his Survival, Evasion, Rescue, and Escape (SERE) training and relying on his two pilot survival kits. Make a list of the items in Captain O'Grady's kit and a list of the items in Brian's survival kit. Circle the items which were found in both. **[Health]**

Choose one survival technique Captain O'Grady used to help him survive and tell how Brian could have used the same technique to help him survive in the Canadian wilderness. **[Health]**

Super Search: Name an edible plant that grows in Bosnia.

5. Internet Public Library

www.ipl.org/youth/AskAuthor/paulsen.html

The Internet Public Library is the first public library on the Internet. The IPL provides free library services to the Internet community including this Web page on the lives of successful authors.

Activity

Read Gary Paulsen's biography. Write a few paragraphs explaining how the experiences in his life may have influenced him in becoming an author of survival stories. **[Language Arts]**

Super Search: How many Newbery Honor winners has Gary Paulsen written?

On Your Own

Canada, bushplanes, pilots, Canadian wildlife, Gary Paulsen, Federal Aviation Administration, Cessna 406, survival, moose

Suggested Reading

Bumford, Sheila. *The Incredible Journey*. Delacorte, 1996. A Labrador retriever, a bull terrier, and a Siamese cat travel miles across the Canadian Wilderness to find their family.

Paulsen, Gary. *Brian's Winter*. Delacorte Press, 1996. Beginning where *Hatchet* might have ended, Brian is forced to survive a winter in the wilderness with only his hatchet and a survival kit.

Paulsen, Gary. *Dogsong*. Bradbury, 1985. A young Eskimo teenager takes a journey by dog sled across the tundra and mountains to search for his identity.

Paulsen, Gary. *Night John*. Delacorte, 1993. Sarny is a twelve-year-old slave who risks her life when a new slave offers to teach her how to read.

Paulsen, Gary. *The River*. Delacorte, 1991. Brian is asked to return to the Canadian wilderness in this sequel to *Hatchet*. Scientists want him to recreate his survival experience so they can learn more about the psychology of survival.

Additional Sources

A Cry in the Wild. MGM Studios, 1990. This 81 minute VHS film is based on the book *Hatchet*.

Devereaux, Elizabeth. "Gary Paulsen." *Publishers Weekly*, Vol. 24, March 28, 1994, pp. 70-71. This is an article about Gary Paulsen and the books he has written.

Whitefeather, Willy. *Outdoor Survival Handbook for Kids*. Harbinger House, 1990. The author advises children on how to survive if they are ever lost in the woods or in the desert.

17

Homer Price
Robert McCloskey • Viking, 1943
Reading Level: 6.5 • 148 pages

Summary

Homer Price is the main character in these six tales about a young boy living in midwestern America. Homer always seems to find himself in humorous situations which include catching thieves with a skunk, operating a magnificent doughnut making machine, and helping to solve the mystery of Michael Murphy's musical mousetrap.

Website Activities

1. National Geographic World Online

www.nationalgeographic.com/features/96/inventions/

National Geographic World Online is written for kids. This particular section offers information, games, and activities on inventions.

Activities

Homer's Uncle Ulysses loved to invent labor-saving machines. Click on the monkey to play the invention games. Be sure to read the instructions carefully before you begin. You will need to have "Shockwave" on your computer for the games to work. **[Science]**

Select "It's Your Turn." Use the "Inventor's Coloring Book" to create your own invention by printing the objects, coloring them, and assembling the parts you choose. Print the invention form and mail it to National Geographic World. Your drawing may be used in National Geographic World or World Online. **[Science, Art]**

Super Search: What is another word for a machine?

2. Wacky Patent of the Month

colitz.com/site/wacky.htm

Michael Colitz is a registered patent attorney with a practice limited to U.S. patent prosecution. He created this site which includes an overview of the patenting process, links to information of interest to inventors, and a "Wacky Patent of the Month."

Activities

Homer's uncle invented a wacky machine to increase doughnut production. Click on the current wacky patent of the month. Select "Prior Wacky Patents" and view actual inventions which have received patents. Pick the invention you think is the silliest and tell why you chose that particular invention. **[Science]**

Select "Patenting" and learn the steps included in the patenting process. Use details from the story to write a disclosure for Uncle Ulysses' automatic doughnut maker. **[Language Arts]**

Super Search: How many years does a patent protect an invention after it is filed?

3. The Pied Piper of Hamelin

www.netten.net/~bmassey/PiedPiper.html

Bill Massey collected his favorite stories and poems. He placed them at this website along with a short biography for each author and poet.

Activity

Mr. Murphy was called a "Pied Piper" in *Homer Price*. Read the actual text of the poem "The Pied Piper" written by Robert Browning. Give examples of how Mr. Murphy was similar to the Pied Piper. **[Language Arts]**

Super Search: Who hired the Pied Piper to get rid of the rats in Hamelin?

4. Garfield Online

www.garfield.com/comics/

Garfield Online is Garfield's official home page. It contains comic strips, trivia, games, and activities.

Activities

Fredy and Homer enjoyed reading the "Super Duper" comic strip in the newspaper every day. Read the Garfield comic strips. If you find a comic strip you enjoy, you can send it to a friend on a comic e-postcard. Check with your teacher before you e-mail your postcard. **[Language Arts]**

Select "Fat Cat Facts" and use these facts to help create your own Garfield comic strip. Use the "Garfield Coloring Book" to help illustrate your comic strip. **[Art]**

Select Garfield's "Video Clips" and view a few episodes of Garfield with his friend. Check with your teacher before you download the files. **[Language Arts]**

Super Search: How much older is Garfield than you?

5. Learn.Com

www.learn2.com/04/0440/0440.html

Learn2.Com is the ability utility website. The site provides tutorials and instructions on a wide variety of topics to make your life easier.

Activity

Michael Murphy wouldn't have needed his musical mousetrap if he had known about this site. Read the instructions for "How to Capture a Mouse." Draw a sketch of your home or apartment and label each room in your drawing. Use the information you learned at this site to find the best locations to place mouse traps. Make an "X" in each area of the house where you would put a trap. Explain why you chose these locations. **[Social Studies, Art]**

Super Search: Name a food which can be used as bait in a mouse trap.

On Your Own

skunks, comic books, Super Heroes, doughnuts, machines, inventions, advertising, collections, hobbies, amnesia, Rip Van Winkle

Suggested Reading

Hurwitz, Johanna. *The Adventures of Ali Baba Bernstein.* Morrow, 1985. David Bernstein wants to have a more exciting life so he decides to change his name to Ali Baba Bernstein.

McCloskey, Robert. *Centerburg Tales.* Viking Press, 1951. Homer Price has more humorous adventures in Centerburg. This time a mad scientist develops weeds which overrun the town.

McCloskey, Robert. *Time of Wonder.* Viking, 1957. Two children have exciting adventures when they spend their summer vacation on an island off the coast of Maine.

Additional Sources

Bender, Lionel. *Eyewitness Books: Inventions.* Knopf, 1991. Lionel Bender provides photographs and text to explore inventions such as the wheel, clocks, and telephones.

Happily Every After: Fairy Tales for Every Child: The Pied Piper. HBO Video, 1998. Robert Guillaume narrates the story of the Pied Piper who mesmerizes the rats and children of Hamlet with his saxophone.

Homer Price Stories. Children's Circle, WWK Associates, 1993. This videotape contains some of Robert McCloskey's most humorous Homer Price stories.

Wright, David K. *Computers.* Marshall Cavendish, 1996. *Computers* discusses the development of modern computers, the ways they are used, and future possibilities for computers.

18

How to Eat Fried Worms
Thomas Rockwell • Bantam Doubleday Dell, 1973
Reading Level: 4.5 • 128 pages

Summary

When Tom is grounded for not eating his mother's salmon casserole, Billy boasts he could eat a bite of anything. His friends make a bet that Billy can't eat fifteen worms, and he accepts the challenge. Billy's mother even helps out by finding creative recipes to disguise the worms.

Website Activities

1. The Yuckiest Site on the Internet

www.yucky.com/worm/

The Yuckiest Site on the Internet is maintained by New Jersey Online. This site has won almost 30 awards for being a "cool" educational site for kids.

Activities

Select "All About Earthworms" and read the facts on 2,700 different kinds of earthworms. Watch the video of a baby earthworm being hatched from a cocoon and see how many hearts a worm has on the "Heartbeat Video." Check with an adult for permission to download the videos before you begin. **[Science]**

Select "Wendell's Cousins" and read the information presented for all five of the featured worms. If you really had to eat a worm, which one would you choose to eat? Write a paragraph explaining your reasons for choosing this particular worm. **[Language Arts]**

Select "Worms as Recyclers" and read about worms breaking down organic matter into valuable nutrients. Learn how to make a worm recycling bin by following the printed instructions. **[Science]**

Super Search: Which part of the worm is a storage compartment for food?

2. All Recipes/Cakes

www.cakerecipe.com/az/WormCake.asp

All Recipes.com is a network of recipe sites for the whole world. This segment of the website lists recipes for all types of cakes.

Activity

Billy tried to find different ways to disguise the worms so it would be easier for him to eat them. Read this recipe for "Worm Cake" (gummi-worms). Select "Recipe Card" to see how a recipe is written. Write your own recipe using gummi worms. Be sure to include the ingredients on the front of the card and the directions on the back of the card. **[Language Arts]**

Super Search: How long does the icing need to set before you can eat the cupcake?

3. U.S. Post Office

www.usps.gov/kids/

The United States Postal Service created this site especially for kids. It includes all sorts of fun and information on stamps.

Activities

Alan was willing to sell his stamp collection if he lost the bet to Billy. Visit the U.S. Post Office and select "Stamp Stomp." To learn how to start a stamp collection, select "Collecting Pictures of History." Choose the type of stamp you would be interested in collecting and list the simple tools you will need to get started on creating a stamp album. **[Language Arts]**

Select "Stamps Alive" and read why certain stamps in the "Archived Stamp" section were created. Read about the historical and outrageous events for each of the featured stamps. Select

"Design a Stamp" and create your own stamp. Write facts about your stamp and tell why you think your stamp should be the next one chosen and printed by the U.S. Postal Office. **[Social Studies, Art]**

Select "Color a Stamp" and have fun "unleashing the artist within." You will need "Shockwave" on your computer to do this activity. **[Art]**

Super Search: What is the name for the object you will need to hold your stamps in place in your stamp album?

4. Poetry for Kids

www.poetry4kids.com/poems.html

Poetry for Kids is a website filled with children's poems written by the author Kenn Nesbitt. Mr. Nesbitt is the author of a book of poetry titled *My Foot Fell Asleep.*

Activity

Tom made up a silly poem about fish to cheer up Billy. Read the funny poetry at this site and choose your favorite to read to the class. Write your own silly poem about worms. **[Language Arts]**

Super Search: Who wrote all of the poems at this site?

5. Kids Health

KidsHealth.org/parent/community/poison_control _center.index.html

The Nemours Foundation presents this Kids Health website with expert information for families on children's health.

Activity

Billy's mother was so worried about him when she found out he had eaten worms. She made Billy's father call the poison control center to see if eating worms is deadly. Find the phone number for the poison control center in your community. Copy the number on a Post-It note and hang it on your refrigerator at home. **[Health]**

Super Search: How many poison control centers are located in your area?

On Your Own

earthworms, stamp collecting, condiments, night crawlers, poetry, hay fever, poison control, recipes, Shea Stadium

Suggested Reading

Rockwell, Thomas. *How to Fight a Girl.* Franklin Watts, 1987. Joe and Alan plan to get revenge on Billy but the plan backfires when Billy becomes best friends with the prettiest girl in the fifth grade, who just happens to be their secret weapon.

————. *How to Get Fabulously Rich.* Franklin Watts, 1990. Billy wins $410,000 in the lottery and his friends claim he owes them a share for helping him play.

Additional Sources

Darling, Lois. *Worms.* Morrow, 1972. Lois Darling explains the behavior and structure of earthworms and describes their importance to animals and plants.

How to Eat Fried Worms. Listening Library, 1991. These two audiocassettes (running time: 2 hrs.) tell the hilarious worm-eating story by Thomas Rockwell.

Patent, Dorothy Hinshaw. *The World of Worms.* Holiday House, 1978. *The World of Worms* discusses a variety of worms, their characteristics and habits, and their usefulness to humans.

19

The Indian in the Cupboard
Lynne Reid Banks • Bantam Doubleday Dell, 1980
Reading Level: 6.0 • 184 pages

Summary

Omri receives a plastic Indian and an old cupboard for his birthday. He is greatly astonished when he finds that objects come alive if they are placed in the cupboard. All goes well with his new Indian pal, Little Bear, until a cowboy is brought to life. Omri helps the two enemies learn how to get along with each other.

Website Activities

1. Pow Wows

www.powwows.com/dancing/index2.html

Paul Gowder, a member of the Georgia tribe of Eastern Cherokees, prepared this site on Pow Wow Dancing. He describes pow wow dance styles and provides information on Native American pow wows.

Activities

Omri promised Little Bear he would get him a wife if the Indian performed a native dance. Read about the different styles of men's pow wow dancing at this site. Select one of the dances and draw a picture of Little Bear dancing. Use the information you learn to dress Little Bear in the proper ceremonial clothing. **[Social Studies]**

Select "What Is a Pow Wow." Learn about the history of pow wows and what occurs at this celebration. Select "Pow Wow Calendar" and write the locations of three pow wows which will be held during this current month on the calendar. **[Social Studies]**

Super Search: What is the name for the parade signifying the beginning of the pow wow?

2. The Soda Fountain

www.sodafountain.com

The Soda Fountain website includes historical information on soft drinks and ice cream. It provides recipes, a forum, and links to your favorite sodas. The site is sponsored by various ice cream and soda companies.

Activities

Select "Soft Drinks" and find the original secret formula for Coca-Cola. List the ingredients which were originally used to make Coke. Select "Robert Goizueta—Changed the Formula" and write a paragraph describing how Mr. Goizueta changed the formula and how the consumers reacted to this change. **[Language Arts]**

Select your favorite soft drink, click on the logo and read the information. Write three new facts you learned about your soda. **[Language Arts]**

Super Search: What was the name of the recipe which contained the original Coca-Cola formula?

3. First Nations

www.dickshovel.com/iro.html

First Nations is a website owned and maintained by Jordan Dill, a Tsalagi (Cherokee) who is also a member of the American Indian Movement. The site is dedicated to honoring Native Americans by providing the history of American Indians and other valuable information.

Activity

Omri had difficulties understanding Little Bear because he didn't know much about the Iroquois' way of life. Scroll through this article on the history of the Iroquois until you find the section on "Culture." Read the information on the social structure and customs of the Iroquois people. What information did you learn that could have helped Omri when he was trying to understand Little Bear? **[Social Studies]**

Super Search: Which noteworthy Iroquois chief served on General Grant's staff during the Civil War and helped to write the terms of Lee's surrender at Appomattox?

4. Brit Speak

pages.prodigy.com/NY/NYC/britspk/ukus1.html

The Brit Speak language laboratory compiled these words for the *British-American Dictionary* online. Many of the words are colloquialisms and words from our *everyday language.*

Activity

Lynn Reid Banks is a British author who includes many British words and phrases in her writing. In the beginning of the book *Indian in the Cupboard*, she even includes a list of some of these British words with the American meanings. Use this "Brit Speak Dictionary" to write five sentences using British words. Underline these words in your sentences. Trade your sentences with a classmate and *see* if he or she can translate them into the American speak. **[Language Arts]**

Super Search: What is the meaning of the underlined word? Little Bear stuck an <u>elastoplast</u> on Boone's chest.

5. Tornado Chase Day

www.chaseday.com/

The purpose of "Tornado Chase Day" is to share ideas and experiences about weather phenomena and several weather events with others interested in storms and storm photography. The site was developed by Gene Moore, an environmental management specialist and avid storm chaser.

Activity

Omri showed Little Bear and Boone a large hailstone. It looked like the size of a football to the tiny characters. Select "Hail and Hailstorms" and then "Hailstones" and take a look at how large some hailstones can be. Find data given for these hailstones and use a ruler or compass to actually draw hailstones to the correct dimensions reported at this site. **[Science]**

Super Search: If you are driving in a car and there is a hailstorm, what should you do?

On Your Own

Iroquois, Indian customs, cowboys, longhouses, Great Britain, scalping, British literature, hallucinations, hailstones, chefs

Suggested Reading

Banks, Lynne. *The Mystery of the Cupboard.* Camelot, 1996. Omri's family moves to the country and Omri discovers many secrets in this sequel to *The Secret of the Indian.*

Banks, Lynne Reid. *The Return of the Indian.* Avon, 1995. Omri helps Little Bear when he is badly wounded during the French and Indian Wars in the sequel to *The Indian in the Cupboard.*

Additional Sources

Doherty, Craig, and Katherine M. Doherty. *The Iroquois.* Franklin Watts, 1989. *The Iroquois* examines the history, customs, religion, lifestyle, and current situation of the Iroquois Indians.

The Indian in the Cupboard. Viacom News Media, 1995. Based on the book, this CD-ROM is an educational game in which you can explore eighteenth-century Iroquois life and traditions.

The Indian in the Cupboard. College Arts Association, 1996. *The Indian in the Cupboard* story is available in VHS format or laser disc.

20

James and the Giant Peach
Roald Dahl • Knopf, 1961
Reading Level: 4.5 • 128 pages

Summary

James becomes an orphan at an early age and is raised by his two miserable aunts. When James discovers a magical peach, he climbs inside it and finds some strange creatures living there. James and his new buddies manage to escape and travel across the ocean. Along the way, they experience numerous problems. James becomes a hero when he continues to find the solutions.

Website Activities

1. Peaches 'n Dreams

www.awn.com/mag/issue1.2/articles1.2/jackson1.2.html

Animal World Magazine is the world's first electronic monthly publication devoted to the art, craft, and industry of animation. This particular Web page is a review of the Disney movie *James and the Giant Peach*. The article is by Wendy Jackson.

Activity

James and the Giant Peach was recreated in a movie directed by Henry Selick. Mr. Selick describes how talented artists created the animated characters in the Disney movie. View the images of the artists' interpretations of the characters. Draw your own illustrations of the following characters—James, the two aunts, grasshopper, spider, glow-worm, centipede, ladybug, and earthworm. **[Art]**

Super Search: What is the name of Roald Dahl's widow?

2. Spider Webs

www.youcan.com/spider/spider.html

Jox Church is a children's author who writes the comic strip/newspaper feature, "You Can with Beakman and Jax." The site presents many puzzling questions which are answered by Beakman and Jax.

Activities

The spider in the story wove webs for the other creatures to use as beds. Do you know why spiders do not get caught in their own webs? Follow the directions on this website and you can complete an experiment which will answer this question.

You can make a spider web collection by following these tips on webbing. Take an adult with you to go webbing. Some spiders are dangerous and you should not look for spider webs alone.

Super Search: What type of web does a black widow spider weave?

3. Kid's Clubhouse

www.eduplace.com/kids/index.html

Kids' Clubhouse is a fun educational site developed by the Houghton Mifflin Company.

Activities

James was excellent at solving problems in *James and the Giant Peach*. Enter the "Kids' Clubhouse" and select "Brain Teasers" to see if you can find solutions to the problems presented on this website. If you have difficulties, check the hints which are provided for each question. **[Language Arts]**

Enter the "Reading Room" and read the author/illustrator spotlight for this month. Write an author spotlight for Roald Dahl. Include a book

summary for *James and the Giant Peach*, a list of other books Dahl wrote, and a short biography on the author's life. To help you write your author spotlight, connect to <www.roalddahl.org>.
[Language Arts]

Super Search: Where was Roald Dahl born?

4. Empire State Building

www.esbnyc.com/html/empire_state_building.html

This is the official home page for the Empire State Building in New York City.

Activity

The giant peach came to rest on the needle of the Empire State Building. Take a virtual tour of this famous skyscraper. Select "Tourism," "Fact," and "History" and read the information given. Then select "Kids' Stuff" and enter the "Kids' Trivia Contest" for a chance to win a free pass to visit the observatories at the Empire State Building. **[Social Studies]**

Super Search: How long did it take to build the Empire State Building?

5. Vapor Trails

www.vaportrails.com/USA/USAFeatures/QueenMary/QueenMary.html

Vapor Trails is an online travel magazine. Cheri Sicard wrote this article called, "A Nostalgic Story." The article describes the Queen Mary and what has happened to her.

Activity

James and the giant peach floated over the Queen Mary as it was sailing out of the English Channel on her way to America. Read the information at this site on how the Queen Mary has been converted into a luxury hotel. Write three ideas you have for making the Queen Mary hotel an even bigger attraction for tourists.
[Social Studies]

Super Search: When was the Queen Mary originally launched?

On Your Own

England, peaches, insects, magic, spider webs, fruits, problem solving, seagulls, Queen Mary, hailstones, rainbows, Empire State Building

Suggested Reading

Dahl, Roald. *The BFG.* Farrar, Straus & Giroux, 1982. The BFG (Big Friendly Giant) is a nice giant who tries to put an end to the loathsome activities of the other giants who eat little boys and girls.

————. *Charlie and the Chocolate Factory.* Cornerstone Books, 1985. Charlie and four other children win a tour of the world's most fantastic chocolate factory.

————. *Danny, the Champion of the World.* Knopf, 1975. Danny is a motherless boy who lives in a gypsy caravan and has a best friend who is full of surprises.

Additional Sources

Bugs: The Complete Interactive Guide to Insects. Inroads Interactive, 1996. This computer optical disc comes with an installation guide sheet. The disc contains over six hundred insects, including butterflies, ants, spiders, and others. Informative articles and audio accompany the colorful photography and video.

George, Richard. *Roald Dahl's Charlie and the Chocolate Factory: A Play.* Knopf, 1976. Five children win a contest to tour the Willy Wonka Candy Factory. Richard George adapted Dahl's book into this play format.

James and the Giant Peach. Disney Films, 1996. This 79-minute video based on Roald Dahl's book was nominated for an Academy Award for best original musical or comedy score.

West, Mark. *Roald Dahl.* Maxwell Macmillan, 1992. Mark West describes Roald Dahl's style of writing in this book which is part of Twaynes' English authors series.

21
Like Jake and Me
Mavis Jukes • Knopf, 1984.
Reading Level: 4.5 • 32 pages

Summary

Alex desperately wants his stepfather to love and accept him. Alex and his stepfather do not have much in common. Alex enjoys taking ballet lessons and studying spiders. Jake is a cowboy and he likes chopping and stacking wood. One day they are drawn together in a humorous situation when Alex shows his "true strength" to his stepdad.

Website Activities

1. Carolina Wolf Spider

www.arizhwys.com/Wildlife/carolinawolfspider. html

The Arizona Department of Transportation features animals of the Southwest desert at this site and provides descriptions of the animals' habitats and behaviors.

Activity

A California wolf spider does not have a poisonous bite but he sure is scary looking. Get a close up look at the type of spider that was climbing on Jake. **[Science]**

Super Search: Which variety of wolf spider is the largest of the species?

2. Arachnology Home Page

www.ufsia.ac.be/Arachnology/Pages/Scientists. html

The Arachnology Home Page is a directory of spider information on the Internet. It provides more than 1,000 links to arachnological sites.

Activity

Alex's father was an entomologist in the story *Like Jake and Me*. This website provides a list of entomologists and arachnologists (scientists who study spiders) from around the world. These scientists have their own websites which provide more information on their jobs and their personal lives. Choose one of the scientists and e-mail him/her with a question you may have about spiders. Share your response with the class. Check with your teacher for permission before you send your e-mail. **[Science]**

Super Search: How many species of arachnids are now extinct?

3. Job Opportunities in Entomology

www.colostate.edu/Depts/Entomology/

This site is operated by the Colorado State University and is the first entomology website in the world.

Activity

Select "Jobs" and look at the list of job opportunities for entomologists. Choose one of the job positions from the list. Tell why you would like to have that particular job. Explain why you would like to live in this region of the United States.
[Social Studies]

Super Search: Which state has the most job opportunities listed in the field of entomology?

4. Stetson's

www.stetsonhat.com/history.htm

This is the official website for Stetson's legendary hats.

Activity

Stetson hats were first made in 1865. Jake and millions of other people wear Stetson hats. Read the history of the Stetson hat. Look at the pictures of some of the hats and caps. Choose one you like and draw a picture of yourself wearing your new Stetson. **[Art]**

Super Search: Where is the Stetson Hat Factory located?

5. American Library Association

www.ala.org/alsc/newbery.html

The American Library Association maintains this site and provides information on all Newbery and Caldecott Award books.

Activities

Like Jake and Me was named as a 1985 Newbery honor book. The Newbery was the first children's book award in the world. Select "About the Medal" and "How It Is Awarded." In a few paragraphs, paraphrase the facts you learn about the Newbery Medal. **[Language Arts]**

Select "Past Winners" and "Honor Books." List the names of the medal-winning books you have read. **[Language Arts]**

Super Search: Write the names of the Newbery Medal and Honor winners for the year you were born.

6. The Male Dancer

www.bravo.ca/footnotes/episodes/episode7.html

Sound Venture Productions is an independent production company specializing in arts, culture, and documentary television programs. This episode is a documentary featuring male ballet dancers.

Activity

Alex was embarrassed to show Jake his ballet moves because he didn't think Jake would appreciate them. Read "The Male Dancer" and learn about the history of a ballet and how it was originally created for men. Compose a letter written from Alex's point of view to Jake explaining why you want to take ballet lessons. Include information you learn at this website. **[Language Arts]**

Super Search: Which infamous group of soldiers took dance lessons as part of their military training?

On Your Own

ballet, cowboys, wolf spider, Stetson, cypress trees, pear trees, ax, entomologist, step parents

Suggested Reading

Adler, C.S. *Her Blue Straw Hat.* Harcourt Brace, 1997. Twelve-year-old Rachel is upset when her stepfather's spoiled daughter goes on vacation with the family.

Boyd, Candy Dawson. *Chevrolet Saturdays.* Macmillan, 1993. Ten-year-old Joey has difficulty accepting his new stepfather because he is still angry about his parents' divorce.

Jukes, Mavis. *I'll See You in My Dreams.* Knopf, 1993. When her seriously ill uncle is in the hospital, a little girl imagines she is a skywriter creating a get well message in the sky.

Jukes, Mavis. *No One Is Going to Nashville.* Knopf, 1983. Sonia's father refuses to let her keep a stray dog until Sonia's stepmother intervenes and convinces him it is a good idea.

Additional Sources

Barysknikov—The Dancer and the Dance. LWT, Ltd., 1982. This 85-minute video is a profile of Barysknikov's life and work. It is narrated by Shirley MacLaine and is part of the Kultur Video Dance Series.

Castor, Harriet. *Ballet Stories.* Kingfisher, 1997. Harriet Castor selected and compiled this collection of fifteen stories about the ballet.

Gibbons, Gail. *Spiders.* Holiday House, 1993. Gail Gibbons examines the behavior, habitats, and physical characteristics of different kinds of spiders.

22

Mr. Popper's Penguins
Florence and Richard Atwater • Little, Brown, 1938
Reading Level: 6.3 • 139 pages

Summary

Mr. Popper is a house painter who studies and dreams about becoming an Antarctic explorer. He writes a letter to Admiral Drake and the Admiral sends him a penguin. The Popper family runs into problems when Mr. Popper receives another penguin and ends up raising a family of ten penguins.

Website Activities

1. The Penguin Page

www.vni.net/~kwelch/penguins/

The Penguin Page is a series of pages containing factual and theoretical information on penguins. The site was created by Kevin C. Welch.

Activities

 Select "Established Species." Make a penguin pictograph for the class to determine which of the seventeen types of penguins shown at this site is the one chosen as the cutest by your classmates. Each classmate should view all of the pictures, pick his/her favorite, draw a picture of it, and glue it on a poster board. **[Science]**

View videos and hear audio clips of each individual species of penguins. You will need "Real Video" on your computer to view the videos.

Make a penguin card game using 3" x 5" index cards. Draw a picture of the penguin on the front of the card. Write the name of the species on the back of the card. See how many penguins your classmates can identify by looking at the pictures on your cards. **[Science, Art]**

Super Search: What is the only member of the megadyptes genus?

2. National Geographic for Kids

www.nationalgeographic.com/kids/

National Geographic for Kids website includes a variety of activities for children.

Activity

Mr. Popper enjoyed reading about expeditions to Antarctica in the National Geographic Magazine. Check out National Geographic for Kids and take the "GEO BEE Challenge." Each day five new geography questions are posted and you can try to answer them correctly to beat the *Bee!* **[Social Studies]**

Super Search: Which grades are eligible to participate in the National Geography Bee sponsored by the National Geographic Society?

3. National Museum of Natural History

www.nmnh.si.edu/arctic/game/

This is the home page for the National Museum of Natural History located at the Smithsonian Institute in Washington, D.C.

Activities

Play "Polar Pairs" and learn about the animals Mr. Popper will see when he explores the Arctic with Admiral Drake. **[Science, Social Studies]**

Open the "Arctic Wildlife Portfolio" to learn more details about arctic animals. There are no penguins in the Arctic but see if you can find an arctic bird that shares some characteristics with penguins. Describe the similarities you discover. **[Science]**

Super Search: How large can a caribou's antlers grow to be?

4. Vaudeville in Ohio

userwww.sfsu.edu/~hl/v.html

This site was created by Hal Layer, professor in the Department of Instructional Technologies at San Francisco State University in California. He compiled this portrait of vaudeville because his great-grandfather managed a vaudeville theater in Willard, Ohio.

Activity

Select "Ads for Chicago Opera House Events." Read the ads which would have appeared at the time Mr. Popper's penguins were performing. Create your own advertisement for Mr. Popper's Penguin Show. **[Language Arts, Art]**

Super Search: How many seats did the original Chicago Opera House contain?

5. Readers on Stage

www.aaronshep.com/rt/ROS.html

Aaron Shepard is an author and storyteller. His website assists students and teachers who are interested in reader's theater.

Activity

Use Mr. Shepard's tips on scripting, staging, and performing a reader's theater. Select a chapter from *Mr. Popper's Penguins* and create a script for your class to perform as a reader's theater. **[Language Arts]**

Super Search: What is the name of the person who tells the story in reader's theater?

6. Glacier

www.glacier.rice.edu/

The National Science Foundation sponsors this site on Antarctica. The site was created by a team of faculty members at Rice University in Houston, Texas.

Activity

Father Popper always wanted to go on an expedition to Antarctica. Select "Expedition" and visit this Web page to learn what it is like to take a journey to the South Pole. Read the information provided for each step in your expedition. Write a letter to Mr. Popper and describe an Antarctic expedition to him. Include the following information:

1. Getting to Antarctica
2. Training at the camp
3. Living at the base station

[Social Studies, Language Arts]

Super Search: How many people travel to Antarctica each year as tourists?

On Your Own

Antarctica, Arctic, penguins, Admiral Drake, performing animals, vaudeville, National Geographic

Suggested Reading

Glimmerveen, Ulco. *A Tale of Antarctica.* Scholastic, 1989. Glimmerveen uses a tale of penguins in Antarctica to demonstrate how their environment is threatened by man and his pollution.

Lester, Helen. *Tacky Penguin.* Houghton Mifflin, 1988. Tacky has a difficult time fitting in with the other penguins until his strange behavior helps to save the lives of his penguin buddies.

Additional Sources

Antarctica. Directed by John Weiley, Finley-Holiday Film Corporation, Lumivision, 1998. This 40-minute documentary film is available in DVD, laser disk, or videocassette.

Geo Bee Challenge. National Geographic CD-ROM. This CD-ROM includes over 2,000 questions from the National Geography Bee.

Somme, Lauritz. *The Penguin Family Book.* Picture Book Studio, 1988. A colony of chinstrap penguins in the Antarctic Ocean are pictured as they lay their eggs, raise the chicks, and watch the chicks become more independent.

Wexo, John Bonnet. *Penguins.* Creative Education, 1990. Zoological consultant, Charles R. Schroder, and scientific consultants, George Gaylord Simpson and Bernard Stonehouse discuss the physical characteristics, habits, behavior, and future of penguins.

23

My Brother Sam Is Dead
James Lincoln Collier and Christopher Collier
Four Winds, 1974
Reading Level: 5.4 • 224 pages

Summary

Tim's brother runs away to fight the British in the Revolutionary War. When Tim's father is attacked and taken to a prison ship, Tim is left at home with his mother to keep their farm and tavern running. Sam returns home and is accused of stealing cattle. Tim and his mother fight valiantly to rescue Sam from being executed after he is court martialed.

Website Activities

1. Kids Can Make a Difference

www.kids.maine.org/

This site is dedicated to Kids Can Make a Difference. The program is educational and focuses on the causes of hunger and poverty and how students can help find solutions to the problems. The program encourages students to take actions in their communities.

Activities

Timothy and the other colonists knew the meaning of hunger because they experienced it. Select "Hunger Facts" and learn about hunger in the United States and throughout the world. Select "Hunger Quiz" and take a short quiz to test your knowledge. **[Social Studies]**

Select "What Kids Can Do" and read the ideas on how you can get involved in making a difference in your community. Choose one of the ideas you would be willing to try or create one of your own ideas. Follow through with the idea you have chosen and develop it into an individual or class project. **[Social Studies]**

Super Search: How many children under the age of twelve in the United States go to bed hungry every night?

2. The "Brown Bess Musket"

www.civilization.ca/cwm/tour/trwe1eng.html

The Canadian War Museum sponsors this site which provides information on numerous weapons of war. The actual museum is located in Ottawa, Ontario.

Activity

Sam stole his father's Brown Bess musket to take with him when he joined the army. Read the information at this site and learn more about the weapon. Write a few paragraphs describing how the Revolutionary War would have been different if the Minutemen had been armed with better weapons. **[Social Studies, Language Arts]**

Super Search: How long did it take an experienced soldier to load and fire a musket?

3. Flags

www.law.ou.edu/flags.html

The University of Oklahoma Law Center sponsors this United States and State Flag Site which was developed and created by Eric Cooper.

Activities

The flags flown during the Revolutionary War are different than the ones we use today. Select "Flags of the U.S." and "Flags of the Revolution." Click on each of the flags to enlarge them so you can see the details better. **[Social Studies]**

Make a State Flags Display in your classroom. Select "Current State Flags" and assign each student in your classroom two or three of the state flags so that every state is selected by someone in the class. Get fifty 5x8" index cards and draw a different state flag on each. Write the name of the state on the back of the index card. Hang the flags on your "State Flags Display" and see how many states you can identify by looking at the pictures of the flags. **[Social Studies, Art]**

Super Search: How many stars were on the 1818 Star Flag?

4. Big Brothers/Big Sisters

www.bbbsa.org/

This is the official home page for the Big Brothers/Big Sisters Association of America.

Activities

Sam could have used a Big Brother when he lost both his father and his brother during the Revolutionary War. The Big Brothers/Big Sisters Association of America was created to provide trusted mentors to children at risk. Select "Stories and Profiles" and read the profiles of outstanding Big Brothers and Big Sisters. Write a few paragraphs telling whether you feel you would make a good volunteer for the organization when you get older. Describe the qualities you feel you possess that would make you a good candidate for the program. **[Language Arts]**

Select "Volunteer! Find an Agency" and read the qualifications needed to become a mentor in the program. Find the agency located nearest your home and write down the phone number. **[Language Arts, Social Studies]**

Super Search: Who was credited with creating the concept of Big Brothers/Big Sisters?

On Your Own

Minutemen, Tories, Loyalists, Lexington, Concord, Fort Ticonderoga, cattle raising, Committee of Safety, Hudson River, sturgeon, prison ships, pewter, hunger, court martials, muskets, Revolutionary War

Suggested Reading

Fritz, Jean, and Lynd Ward. *Early Thunder.* Coward McCann, 1967. Fourteen-year-old Daniel re-examines his loyalty to the King when conflicts arise between the Tories and the Patriots.

Gilman, Dorothy. *The Bells of Freedom.* Macrae Smith, 1963. Jed Crane is an English boy, sold against his will as an indentured servant. Jed escapes from his master and is captured by the rebels when he slips through British lines.

Goodman, Joan Elizabeth. *Hope's Crossing.* Houghton Mifflin, 1998. Hope's father is fighting in the war when Tories kidnap her from her Connecticut home and take her to Long Island.

Additional Sources

American History: Birth of a Nation: Lexington, Concord, and Independence. AIMS Media, 1988. This 16-minute videocassette chronicles the Battles of Lexington and Concord during the Revolutionary War.

Carter, Alden R. *The American Revolution.* Franklin Watts, 1995. Alden Carter discusses the causes, events, and personalities of the American Revolutionary War.

My Brother Sam Is Dead. Rhache Publishing Ltd., 1989. This VHS video is based on the book *My Brother Sam Is Dead.*

24

My Side of the Mountain
Jean George • Scholastic, 1959
Reading Level: 5.9 • 177 pages

Summary

Sam's great grandfather owned land in the Catskill Mountains. Sam decides to find the land and live alone in the woods. He relies on his instincts and his ingenuity for survival. His only companion is a duck hawk falcon. Sam finds shelter in a decayed tree trunk and battles the elements as he struggles to survive a brutal winter in the Catskills.

Website Activities

1. Hiking Trails in the Catskill Mountains

www.catskillguide.com/hikeright.htm

The information at this site is provided by the New York State Department of Environmental Conservation.

Activities

Take a virtual hike through the Catskill Mountains and you will be able to enjoy the same scenery Sam did when he lived in these mountains. Write five facts you learn about the trees and plants in the Catskills while you are "hiking" on the trails. **[Science, Language Arts]**

Select "Weather Forecasts" and view the current weather conditions on Hunter Mountain in the Catskills. Compare the weather conditions given at this site with the conditions you are experiencing in your location. Compare the forecasts for the next few days. **[Science]**

Super Search: How many forest fires are caused by human carelessness?

2. Woodall

www.woodalls.com/tents/advice/fire.html

Woodall is a company which provides people with accurate, up-to-date RV and camping information. This site also contains a directory of camping locations and destinations.

Activity

Sam was distressed because he could not start a fire. Read the expert's advice on how to build a fire by using branches and twigs from deciduous and coniferous trees. Look at the list of trees and write the names of trees which could be found in the woods nearest your city. If you have trees near your home, bring two examples of deciduous and two of coniferous trees to class. **[Science, Social Studies]**

Super Search: How many forest fires are caused by human carelessness?

3. North Carolina Falconer's Guild

www.mindspring.com/~gyrfalcon/ncfg.htm

This site is owned by the North Carolina Falconer's Guild. The guild disseminates information on all raptorial birds. It promotes methods for the care, welfare, and training of raptors.

Activities

Sam was able to train a wild falcon but falconry is time-consuming and is highly regulated. Read the regulations against keeping a falcon. Determine whether you think you would be dedicated enough to become a falconer. If you would like more information, write to the address provided at this site. **[Language Arts]**

Select "Images" of falcons. Choose one of the pictures and use your imagination to write a short descriptive paragraph telling what you think is happening in the picture. **[Language Arts]**

Super Search: What score is required on the falconry test before you may become a falconer?

4. Boy Scouts of America

www.bsa.scouting.org/nav/scouts.html

This is the official website for the Boy Scouts of America.

Activities

Read the "Scout Tips" and tell which tips would have been helpful to Sam as he struggled to survive the winter in the Catskills. **[Health, Social Studies]**

Try the "Morse Code Translator." Write a message in Morse code and see if one of your classmates can translate the message. **[Language Arts]**

Look at the images of the state flags. Have a contest to see who can name the most flags. **[Social Studies]**

Take the "Weather Sign Quiz" and test your knowledge of forecasting the weather. **[Science]**

Super Search: What is required in order to send a semaphore code?

5. Ways to Begin a Journal Writing Practice

www.rio.com/~wplace/howjournal.html

Journal Writer is a monthly newsletter which creates lessons designed for personal growth through journal writing. Click on the pen at the bottom of the page to see the lessons.

Activity

Sam kept a journal when he was surviving in the mountains. Read these tips on how to write a journal. Use the information you learn at this site to write journal entries Sam might have made when his family came to live with him at the end of the story. **[Language Arts]**

Super Search: What should be your first step in the journal writing process?

On Your Own

weasel, Catskill Mountains, duck hawk, whittling, crayfish, mushrooms, hunting, snares, libraries, falcons, fire wardens, training birds, tanning deer-skin, Daniel Boone, vitamin deficiencies

Suggested Reading

George, Jean. *On the Far Side of the Mountain.* Dutton, 1990. This sequel to *My Side of the Mountain* tells the story of Sam's sister running away from home and Sam's pet falcon being confiscated by the game warden.

Holman, Felice. *Slakes's Limbo.* Scribner, 1974. Thirteen-year-old Aremis Slake is bothered by his misfortune so he leaves home and tries to survive by living in New York City's subway tunnels.

Paulsen, Gary. *Brian's Winter.* Delacorte, 1996. Brian is forced to survive a winter in the wilderness with only his hatchet and a survival pack.

Speare, Elizabeth George. *Sign of the Beaver.* Houghton Mifflin, 1983. Local Indians help a young boy to survive when he is left alone to guard his family's home in the wilderness in Maine.

Additional Sources

McManners, Hugh. *The Complete Wilderness Training Book.* Houghton Mifflin, 1994. Hugh McManners provides valuable information on surviving in the wilderness with this training manual.

Olsen, Penny. *Falcon's and Hawks.* Facts on File, 1992. This book describes the characteristics and behavior of falcons and hawks around the world.

My Side of the Mountain. Paramount Home Video, 1969. This videotape based on the story is 100-minutes long and is rated G.

25

Night of the Twisters
Ivy Ruckman • Thomas Y. Crowell, 1984
Reading Level: 6.9 • 153 pages

Summary

Dan and his best friend, Arthur, are babysitting for Dan's baby brother when a tornado hits his Grand Island, Nebraska, home. The children seek shelter in the basement and huddle in the shower stall as the tornado rages overhead. After the tornado, the boys have to locate their family members by maneuvering through the devastated remains of the town.

Website Activities

1. Weather.com

www.weather.com/education/resources/index.html

Weather Channel Enterprises, Inc. owns and operates this site which provides various sources of weather information.

Activities

Select "Backyard Meteorology" and set up your own backyard meteorology station in your schoolyard or in your backyard. Draw a sketch of your weather station and be sure to include all of the necessary equipment. Use the information you learn at this site to help you determine the best locations in which to place your instruments for accurate readings of the weather. **[Science]**

Select "Become a Meteorologist" and read the list of job opportunities available for meteorologists. If you see a job that interests you, click on the links to obtain more information. **[Science]**

Super Search: What are the two types of barometers used by forecasters to measure atmospheric pressure?

2. Wild Weather

www.caps.ou.edu/CAPS/teachwild.html

This site is funded by the Center for Analysis and Prediction of Storms and it provides resources for teachers and scientific activities for children. The Center is located at the University of Oklahoma.

Activities

Special Note: You must have adult permission and supervision for this activity!

Make your own lightning. You will need disposable plastic cups, aluminum foil, and a balloon. Follow the directions for this scientific experiment and you will see how lightning is a discharge of static electricity. **[Science]**

Create your own tornado. For this experiment, you will need a large plastic soft drink bottle with cap, water, dishwashing liquid, and marbles or pebbles. If you follow the directions carefully, the bottle will form a visible funnel in the center which looks like a real tornado. **[Science]**

Super Search: How can you determine the distance to a lightning bolt by listening to the thunder?

3. Happy Days

www.geocities.com/TelevisionCity/9835/

Todd Fuller hosts this site on everything you ever wanted to know about *Happy Days*. Much of the information is taken from *The Complete Directory to Prime Time Network TV Shows* by Tim Brooks and Earle Marsh.

Activities

Dan and Arthur watched *Happy Days* on TV. *Happy Days* was one of the most popular television shows in the late 1970s and into the 1980s. Select "Show Info" and learn about the characters and story lines from the show. Select

"Sound Files" and "Video Clips" and you can actually hear and see episodes from *Happy Days*. **[Language Arts]**

Select "Trivia." You probably do not know the answers to many of these questions, but your parents and grandparents might enjoy answering them. Write your own trivia questions for a television show that is popular today. Have a trivia contest in your classroom and see who can answer the most questions. **[Language Arts]**

Super Search: How many years was *Happy Days* on television?

4. Historical Fiction Criticism and Evaluation

raven.jmu.edu/~ramseyil/histfic.htm

This site is maintained by the Internet School Library Media Center. It is a James Madison University site which provides links of possible interest to librarians and teachers in the electronic library.

Activity

Read "What Is Historical Fiction?" and use this information to write a few paragraphs explaining why *Night of the Twisters* is an example of historical fiction. **[Language Arts, Social Studies]**

Super Search: Name another author who writes historical fiction.

5. The Grand Island Independent

www.theindependent.com/Weather/index.html

The Grand Island Independent newspaper publishes this site in co-operation with the Associated Press.

Activity

We know what the weather in Grand Island, Nebraska, was like on June 4, 1980. Look at this site and write a weather report for the current conditions in Nebraska. Click on the Doppler Radar map to enlarge it. Use a United States map to help you report on the cities where the heaviest precipitation can be found at the current time. **[Science, Social Studies]**

Super Search: In which specific location are the weather conditions in Grand Island recorded?

On Your Own

Grand Island, Nebraska, tornadoes, FEMA, Associated Press, hailstones, historical fiction, Hopi Indians, Civil Defense Emergency, Cornhuskers, National Guard

Suggested Reading

Byars, Betsy. *Tornado*. HarperCollins, 1996. A family waits out a tornado in the storm cellar and the farmhand tells stories about how he found a dog during a tornado when he was a boy.

Ruckman, Ivy. *This Is Your Captain Speaking*. Walker, 1987. A young boy skips soccer practice to visit a nursing home, and he develops a friendship with a retired sea captain.

Additional Sources

Bluestein, Howard B. *Violence in the Skies: The Storms of Tornado Alley*. Oxford University Press, 1998. This nonfiction book includes bibliographical references and an index on tornadoes which ravage the area of the U.S. known as Tornado Alley.

Everything Weather. Sunburst Communications, 1996. Everything Weather is a multimedia interactive experience for grades 5 and up. It includes a video of weather phenomena and has fascinating fact-filled animated sequences. A resource guide and handouts for students are included in the package.

Twister. Warner Home Video, 1996. *Twister* is a 113-minute film based on the book *Night of the Twisters*. It is rated PG-13 and is available on VHS, laser disc, or DVD.

26

Owls in the Family
Farley Mowat • Bantam, 1961
Reading Level: 4.0 • 96 pages

Summary

Billy lives with two owls and a dog in Saskatchewan. The two owls have completely different personalities. Wol terrorizes people and brings dead skunks to the dinner table. Weeps is very comical and is afraid to learn how to fly. Billy has many interesting adventures in Canada with his two most unusual pets and his dog.

Website Activities

1. Raptor Facts

www.raptor.cvm.umn.edu/raptor/rfacts/ghowl.html

The Raptor Center at the University of Minnesota strives to offer a wide range of material on endangered and threatened birds and the environmental issues which affect them. This site provides information for an audience from K-12 students to veterinary medical professionals.

Activities

Learn how to identify a horned owl by reading the facts given on horned owls, looking at a picture of one, and listening to a horned owl's song. **[Science]**

Select "Back to the Raptor Facts Species List" and "Habitat" sections. Read the raptor facts for each bird. Write the names of the raptors which could exist in the environment in your part of the country. **[Science]**

Super Search: In which month does the horned owl lay her eggs?

2. The WatchList

www.audubon.org/bird/watch/list.html

The National Audubon Society sponsors The WatchList. It identifies North American bird species needing our help. The list is compiled by Partners in Flight, a coalition of state, federal, and private sector conservationists who work together to protect the birds of the western hemisphere.

Activities

Select "Kids' WatchList Action." Read the suggestions given on how you can help WatchList birds. Follow the directions for making WatchList trading cards and trade them with your friends. Share other suggestions you would be willing to try in order to help protect threatened birds. **[Science, Art]**

There is a category for owls on the WatchList. Write the names of the owls currently on the list. Tell why these owls are in danger of becoming extinct. **[Science]**

Super Search: Which category of birds has the greatest number of endangered species on the WatchList?

3. Virtual Cave

www.goodearth.com/virtcave.html

The United States Show Cave Directory helps you explore the world of caves at this site. The site offers a complete guide of caves which are open to the public in the United States.

Activities

In the summer, the boys would build a cave along the Saskatchewan River. Take a virtual field trip through a cave and see images of the mineral wonders you would find if you were exploring a cave. **[Science]**

Select "United States Show Caves." Learn more about caves located near your hometown. Read descriptions of the caves and choose one you would like your class to visit. **[Social Studies]**

Super Search: What are "soda straws" called when they continue to grow?

4. Farley Mowat

alvin.lbl.gov/bios/Mowat.html

Farley Mowat is featured on this site as a well-known Canadian author. The biographical information on Mowat's life is furnished by *The Canadian and World Encyclopedia* by McClelland and Stewart.

Activity

Farley Mowat is the author of *Owls in the Family*. Read the information about Mr. Mowat and write a few paragraphs telling how the author's life is similar to Billy's life in the story.
[Language Arts]

Super Search: Which Farley Mowat book was produced as a film?

5. OWL (Orphaned Wildlife Rehabilitation Society)

www.realm.ca/owl/index.html

This is the official World Wide Website of OWL (Orphaned Wildlife Rehabilitation Society) for birds of prey located in British Columbia, Canada.

Activities

Wol and Weeps might have found themselves at this rehabilitation center in Canada. Read the goals of the society and learn what OWL does for injured and orphaned birds of prey. Select "Volunteers" and choose a position you would be willing to serve in if you lived near the center.
[Science]

Select "Adoptions" and then "Boris and Blinkey—Great Horned Owls." Make a list of comparisons among Wol, Weeps, Boris, and Blinkey. **[Language Arts]**

Super Search: How much would it cost to adopt both Boris and Blinkey?

On Your Own

Saskatchewan, owls, gophers, Chinook, veterinarians, pet tricks, caves, crows, Canada, bluffs, cottonwood trees, training birds

Suggested Reading

Mowat, Farley. *The Dog Who Wouldn't Be.* Little, Brown, 1957. Mutt is a marvelous dog who enjoys wearing goggles and riding in open cars.

————. *Lost in the Barrens.* Little, Brown, 1956. Two brothers are stranded in the Canadian Arctic Wilderness when their canoe is destroyed by the rapids. They must learn to survive with neither food nor hope of being rescued.

————. *Never Cry Wolf.* Bantam, 1963. Farley Mowat observes and tracks the activities of a wolf family in the Arctic.

————. *A Whale for the Killing.* Bantam, 1972. A heroic battle is waged to save the life of a whale when it becomes trapped in a lagoon.

Additional Sources

Last Train Across Canada. Acorn Media, 1995. These two VHS tapes are a 110-minute documentary on Murray Sayles's travels across Canada. He traveled over 7,000 miles on the final ride of Canada's cross-country rail line.

Levert, Suzanne. *Saskatchewan.* Chelsea House, 1991. Suzanne Levert discusses the history, culture, and geography of the Canadian province of Saskatchewan. Photographs of Saskatchewan are provided.

Stone, Lynn M. *The Great Horned Owl.* Crestwood House, 1986. Lynn Stone examines the physical characteristics, habitat, life cycle, and behavior of the horned owl.

27

The Pinballs
Betsy Byars • Harper and Row, 1977
Reading Level: 4.2 • 136 pages

Summary

Carlie, Harvey, and Thomas J are sent to live at the Masons' house when they are placed in foster care. The children are strangers to each other and are bitter and unhappy about their new "situation." However, Mr. and Mrs. Mason help them to be more understanding and compassionate.

Website Activities

1. Mothers Against Drunk Driving

www.madd.org

This is the home page for "Mothers Against Drunk Driving." MADD is a nonprofit organization which looks for effective solutions to drunk driving and underage drinking problems. The organization offers support to victims of these crimes.

Activity

Harvey's dad was drunk when he drove over Harvey's legs and broke them. Mothers Against Drunk Driving has been working hard to stop drunk driving and to support victims like Harvey. Select "Statistics" and view the statistics for fatalities by state for the past three years. Make five observations by comparing the results from these three years. **[Math]**

Super Search: How many times are men more likely to drink and drive than women?

2. The Reading Corner

ccpl.carr.lib.md.us/read/

The Reading Corner is a place to find good books to read for students in grades 2–8. It was created by Mona Kerby and is sponsored by the Carroll County Public Library in Westminster, Maryland.

Activity

Harvey and Carlie enjoyed making lists. They also enjoyed going to the library and reading books. Check out "The Reading Corner" and look at the lists of book reviews for young readers. Read some of the reviews and choose three books—one each for Harvey, Carlie, and Thomas J. Make your choices based upon the character traits and interests of each child. Give your reasons for selecting these three particular books. (Special note: There is a book review for *The Pinballs* in the fiction list.) **[Language Arts]**

Super Search: Name two other books written by Betsy Byars.

3. The History Channel

www.historychannel.com/

The History Channel maintains this site which offers events which have occurred on specific dates in history.

Activities

Thomas J and Carlie made Harvey's birthday special by visiting him on his birthday and giving him a puppy. Select "This Day in History" and locate your birthdate. Read all of the fascinating events in history which occurred on your birthday. **[Social Studies]**

Read the "Birthday Board" for your birthdate. This is a list of famous people who were born on your birthday. Select the names of three people who are still living. Tell how old these people are today. **[Social Studies, Math]**

Select the birthdate of one of your relatives who will be celebrating a birthday soon. Copy some of the events which occurred on this date and use the information to make a special "Birthdate" card for this person. **[Social Studies, Art]**

Super Search: Find a song that was popular on the day you were born.

4. Twinspace

www.twinspace.com/

Twinspace is a website that is a resource for and about twins. It provides research on twins, FAQs about twins, and information on twin organizations. The site is maintained by Gilia and Bryony Angell and is hosted by Drizzle.com.

Activity

Thomas J was abandoned on a road and raised by two elderly women—the Benson twins. Read the misconceptions people believe about twins at this site. Select "Twin Interview of the Month" and use the information you learn to write a set of questions you could use if you had the opportunity to interview the Benson women. Think of questions you might like to ask them concerning their past or their lives spent together as twins. **[Language Arts]**

Super Search: Which astrological symbol represents twins?

5. Betsy Byars Home Page

www.betsybyars.com/

Betsy Byars created her own website which includes an autobiography, photos, and writing tips.

Activities

Select "Writing Tips" and read Betsy Byars's valuable lessons on how to succeed as a writer. One of her tips is to write "what you know." Make a list of subjects you would be able to use in your writings because you know these topics well. **[Language Arts]**

Betsy Byars shared her strengths and weaknesses in writing. Give some thought as to what your strengths and weaknesses are. Then write a few paragraphs describing the steps you feel you should take to become a better writer. **[Language Arts]**

Super Search: Which book written by Betsy Byars won the Newbery Medal in 1971?

On Your Own

foster homes, pinball machines, drunk driving accidents, *Guinness Book of World Records*, book lists, nursing careers, Betsy Byars, puppies, twins, fast food, birthday parties, barbershops, cake decorating

Suggested Reading

Byars, Betsy. *Summer of the Swans*. Viking, 1970. A teenage girl feels remorse when she loses patience with her mentally retarded brother and he gets lost in the woods.

Paterson, Katherine. *The Great Gilly Hopkins*. Crowell, 1978. Gilly is put in yet another foster home and tries to cope with her feelings of loneliness and abandonment.

Additional Sources

Crisfield, Deborah. *Update: Drinking and Driving*. Crestwood House, 1995. Deborah Crisfield discusses various efforts to reduce the incidence of drunk driving. This book is written for readers who are ages 9–12.

Gay, Kathlyn.*Adoptions and Foster Care* . Enslow, 1990. *Adoptions and Foster Care* describes how young people feel when they are placed in homes through adoption or foster care.

The Pinballs. Listening Library, 1988. Betsy Byars's *The Pinballs* is told on two audiocassettes.

28

Rascal
Sterling North • Puffin, 1963
Reading Level 5.0 • 189 pages

Summary

Eleven-year-old Sterling raises an abandoned baby raccoon when he finds the animal in the woods. Rascal becomes his constant companion and they go fishing and camping together. When Rascal gets bigger, Sterling has to decide whether to keep him or release him and let Rascal go free.

Website Activities

1. Raising Raccoons

www.loomcom.com/raccoons/info/raising-raccoons.html

This is the World Wide Raccoon Website. It features raccoon facts and information, raccoons in the news, raccoon links, and an interactive bulletin board dedicated to the discussion of raccoons. This award-winning site is produced by Seth J. Morabito, a self-professed "raccoon fan."

Activity

Sterling raised Rascal because he was abandoned by his mother. Raccoons do not make good pets because they demand so much attention. Read this article written on raising raccoons and make a list of the "top ten" tips you should know if you decide to keep a raccoon as a pet. **[Science, Language Arts]**

Super Search: What colors are the eyes of a baby raccoon?

2. Ricky Raccoon

www.toto-cgi.com/playground/ricky/index.html

This site was created by Toto, a multimedia consultancy firm offering strategic solutions to corporations. It also develops educational multimedia titles for school and consumer markets.

Activities

Join the "Adventures of Ricky Raccoon" by selecting "Dressing Game." Dress Ricky by clicking on a piece of clothing and dragging it to Ricky. Dress Heidi Hedgehog when you are finished dressing Ricky. You will need to have "Shockwave" on your computer to play the Dressing Game. **[Art]**

Select "Ricky's Song" and listen to Ricky Raccoon sing. You will need to have "Quick Time" for the song to load to your computer. **[Music]**

Select "Puzzle Games." There are four puzzles available. Click on the scene Sterling and Dad would have seen when they were camping and fishing in the woods. Click and drag the pieces to unscramble the puzzle. This activity also requires your computer to have "Shockwave." **[Language Arts]**

Super Search: Name two of Ricky's favorite sports.

3. The Great Lakes

www.great-lakes.net/places/watsheds/grlakes.html

The Great Lakes Information Network's website provides information relating to the Great Lakes region of North America. GLIN offers a wealth of data and information about the region's environment, economy, tourism, education, and more.

Activity

Sterling lived near the largest of the Great Lakes—Lake Superior. Read the Great Lakes facts at this site. Get five 8-1/2"x 11" sheets of paper. Sketch the shape of one of the Great Lakes on one piece of paper. Make the shape large enough so that you have enough room inside the drawing to write five details you learn about the lake. Repeat these steps for the other four lakes. Cut out each lake, arrange them in correct geographical order (as they appear on a map), and glue them on a poster board. When you are finished, you will have a poster displaying 25 facts on the Great Lakes. **[Social Studies, Art]**

Super Search: Which river links Lake Erie with Lake Ontario?

4. Time Service Department

tycho.usno.navy.mil/time.html

The Department of the Navy maintains this site which records the current time as reported on the Master Clock in Washington, D.C.

Activity

*When Sterling and Rascal were in the woods, Sterling had no watch and could only guess at time by looking at the sun. The Department of the Navy serves as the country's official time keeper. The Navy has a Master Clock facility located at the Washington Naval Observatory in Washington, D.C. Copy the current time as measured by the Master Clock. Compare this time to the time on your classroom clock. Tell the difference in hours, minutes, and seconds. Special note: The hour may not be the same because of the difference in time zones. **[Science]**

Super Search: What is the name for the new atomic clock being developed?

5. The Locker Room

members.aol.com/msdaizy/sports/swim.html

This site provides sports information for kids, including sports facts and helpful tips on participating in sports activities. S. Poole produces this site which has been rated "For All Ages" by "SafeSurf."

Activities

Sterling and his father enjoyed swimming with Rascal in a stream. Sterling was proud because he had learned to do the Australian crawl. Select "The History of Swimming" and learn how swimming

grew to be a competitive sport. Make a list to show which cultures valued swimming in their societies. Start with prehistoric man and list each group in chronological order. **[Social Studies, Health]**

Swimmers should do basic stretches before entering the water. Select "Swimming Warm-Ups" and practice these exercises. Draw a sketch of a stick figure demonstrating the correct way to do one of the exercises. **[Health, Art]**

Super Search: When did swimming become a sport in the Olympics?

On Your Own

raccoons, fly fishing, canoes, autobiographies, burial mounds, Great Lakes, loons, telling time, taxidermy, tobacco farming, rabies

Suggested Reading

Leslie, Robert Franklin. *Ringo, the Robber Raccoon: The True Story of a Northwoods Rogue.* Dodd, Mead, 1984. The author writes about his friendship with a wild raccoon in the British Columbia wilderness.

Additional Sources

The Adventures of Ricky Raccoon – Lost in the Woods. Thomas Learning Tools, 1996. This CD-ROM is a multimedia reading enrichment program for children. It provides interactive games and stories on vocabulary and comprehension.

MacClintock, Dorcas. *A Natural History of Raccoons.* Scribner, 1981. Dorcas MacClintock discusses the characteristics and behavior of raccoons and includes a section on the relatives of the raccoon.

Nentl, Jerolyn Ann. *The Raccoon.* Crestwood House, 1984. *The Raccoon* describes the habits, behavior, physical characteristics, and environment of the raccoon.

Rascal. Listening Library, 1998. This is an audio-cassette version of the book by Sterling North.

29

Ribsy
Beverly Cleary • Bantam Doubleday Dell, 1964
Reading Level: 5.3 • 192 pages

Summary

When the Huggins family travels to the local shopping mall, Ribsy—the family dog, jumps out of the car and becomes disoriented. Another family believes he has been abandoned so they take Ribsy home. Ribsy begins his quest to return home but he keeps getting adopted by other people because he is so lovable. Meanwhile, Henry Huggins is placing lost dog ads in the newspaper and scouring the town for his beloved dog.

Website Activities

1. Pet Action League

www.petrescue.com/

The Pet Action League of Florida created this site because it believes all animals deserve to be treated humanely and with respect. The site offers valuable pet tips, pet rescue information, and links to other pet resources.

Activities

Henry Huggins placed an advertisement in the newspaper for his lost dog. Select "Lost Pet Tips" and read the tips at this site for locating a lost dog. List the ideas from this article that Henry could have used in trying to find Ribsy. List the ideas Henry would not have found helpful in his situation. **[Language Arts]**

Select "Tails to Tell" and read the "stories" these pets wrote from their own point of view. Write a story Ribsy would tell from his point of view describing his adventures and experiences. **[Language Arts]**

Super Search: Name three pieces of information which should be found on your dog's collar tag.

2. Human Left-Handedness

pages.nyu.edu/~whl203/lefty/tests.htm#return

This Human Left-handedness Web page aims to raise consciousness about issues of special concern for left-handed people. The site provides information, history, and other interesting aspects of human left-handedness.

Activity

Henry knew Ribsy was left-handed (left-pawed) because the dog shook hands with his left paw. Take these simple tests to determine your handedness. Do a survey in your class and chart the results. Chart the percentages of students in your class who are left-handed, footed, eyed, and/or eared. Compare your class chart to the statistics comparison table at this site and explain the differences. **[Social Studies, Math]**

Super Search: According to this article, what percentage of all people are strongly right-handed?

3. Peanuts

www.unitedmedia.com/comics/peanuts/

This is the official Peanuts website designed by United Media.

Activities

Read about the life of another dog. This dog happens to be very famous worldwide. Select "History" and follow the timeline for Snoopy and his creator, Charles Schulz. Find the entry on the timeline for the year you were born. **[Social Studies]**

Select the "Strip Library" and view several of Charles Schulz's strips from the past. Draw your own comic strip and include Ribsy with Snoopy or one of the other characters from Snoopy's family. **[Art]**

Super Search: When was the first Peanuts' comic strip published?

4. Multnomah County Library's Kids Page

www.multnomah.lib.or.us/lib/kids/cleary.html

This Web page is the Multnomah County Library's Kids Page. It is produced in Portland, Oregon, by the MCL Youth Services Department. The site describes the Beverly Cleary Sculpture Garden for Children.

Activity

Beverly Cleary was born and raised in Oregon. A Beverly Cleary Sculpture Garden for children has been built to honor the popular children's author. The garden is located in Portland's Grant Park near the actual Klickitat Street. View the bronze statues of Henry Huggins and Ribsy. Write a letter to Beverly Cleary and tell her how you enjoyed her book—*Ribsy*. The address is listed on this site. Have your teacher help you edit your letter before you send it. **[Language Arts]**

Super Search: What was the name of the Portland artist who sculpted the bronze statues?

5. Office of the Fire Marshal

www.gov.nb.ca/mch/ofm.htm

The Government of New Brunswick in Canada developed this site to help people prepare a fire escape plan in the event of a fire.

Activity

Ribsy was trapped on a fire escape and had problems getting down. Fire escapes provide an escape route in apartment buildings in case of a fire. Every home should have its own escape route plan. Read how you can develop a fire escape plan for your home. Draw a floor plan of your home and show all possible exits from each room.

Discuss the escape plan with your family and practice the plan so every family member knows what to do. **[Health]**

Super Search: What should you do before you open a door when you are involved in a fire?

On Your Own

bloodhounds, dog grooming, SPCA, left-handedness, newspaper headlines, elevators, fire escapes, finding a lost pet, fleas, newspaper ads

Suggested Reading

Cleary, Beverly. *Dear Mr. Henshaw.* Morrow, 1983. Ten-year-old Leigh writes letters to his favorite author that divulge his feelings about his parents' divorce.

———. *Ralph S. Mouse.* Morrow, 1982. A motorcycle-riding mouse goes to school and begins an investigation of the other rodents in school.

Taylor, Theodore. *The Trouble with Tuck.* Doubleday, 1981. A young girl wants to help her blind dog so she obtains a seeing-eye dog companion and trains her dog to follow him.

Additional Sources

Homeward Bound: The Incredible Journey. Walt Disney Home Video, 1997. *Homeward Bound* is based on the story of three pets who traveled 250 miles across Canada to find their homes and families. The movie is available in VHS or DVD format and is rated "G."

National Geographic Video. Those Wonderful Dogs. Columbia Tri-Star Home Video, 1995. This 60-minute videocassette is a tribute to dogs around the world.

30

Sing Down the Moon
O'Dell, Scott • Dell, 1970
Reading Level: 5.3 • 137 pages

Summary

Two young Navajo girls are tending sheep when they are kidnapped by Spaniards and forced into slavery. The girls manage to escape and return to their Navajo families. Not much time passes before white soldiers invade their Indian village, destroy their homes, and burn their crops. The Indians are forced to travel to Fort Sumner on what has become known as "The Long Walk" across Arizona. The Navajos are held as prisoners at the fort until they are finally released to return to their homeland.

Website Activities

1. Cyberwest Magazine

www.cyberwest.com/15adwst4.html

This is an article written for *Cyberwest Magazine* by author Maryann Gaig.

Activity

Read this article and take a guided tour through Canyon de Chelly with a Navajo guide named Lupita. After you complete your tour, write five questions you would like to ask Lupita. The questions should either be about the Navajo culture or Navajo life in the Canyons. **[Social Studies]**

Super Search: When did humans first inhabit the canyons?

2. Canyon de Chelly

www.desertusa.com/ind1/du_cdc_main.html

Desert USA is a monthly Internet-based magazine that is a travel and recreation guide to the American Southwest.

Activities

Take a virtual field trip to Canyon de Chelly National Monument and view a hogan similar to the ones in which the Navajos lived. **[Social Studies]**

Use the information at this site to make your own postcard. Cut a piece of oaktag or railroad board to 5"x8". Draw a picture of a scene from Canyon de Chelly on the front of the card. On the back of the card, tell your friend about the marvelous vacation you are having at the Canyon and include details you learn by reading the information at this site. **[Social Studies, Art]**

Super Search: On which day of the week is Navajo Day celebrated?

3. Navajo Nation

www.americanwest.com/pages/navajo2.htm

This site is a presentation of the history and development of the American West, from the frontier and pioneer days of the Wild West to today's modern West. The late Bengt Lindeblad researched the information on this site which is a celebration of all pioneers and pathfinders.

Activity

Explore the Navajo Nation at this site. Read how the lives of the Navajo Indians have changed since the time of "The Long Walk." Make a list of the traditions which have survived for the Navajo. **[Social Studies, Language Arts]**

Super Search: What percentage of Navajos are twenty-four years old or younger?

4. Museum of Science

www.mos.org/sln/toe/toe.html

This site belongs to the Museum of Science in Boston. It contains a list of the museum's current exhibits and programs. The site also provides research and links for teachers.

Activities

🖱 Bright Morning's brother was killed when he was struck by lightning. Select "Safety Quiz" and take the quiz to learn more about lightning. Check your answers to see how much you have learned. [Health, Science]

🖱 Select "Franklin's Kite" and read the information on Benjamin Franklin's famous experiment with lightning. Click on "video clip" and view a video of a kite being struck by lightning. **Never** try an experiment with electricity on your own. These types of experiments are extremely dangerous and should only be done in science laboratories under close supervision. [Science]

Super Search: What is the name for the device which is used for collecting electricity?

5. Animal Tracking Cards

www.princeton.edu/~oa/trackcar.html

This article was written by Rick Curtis, director of the Outdoor Action program at Princeton University.

Activity

🖱 The Navajo were careful to cover their horse's tracks so the Spaniards could not follow them. Print a copy of the Animal Tracking Cards at this site. The cards show the basic track shape, standard walking gait, and basic facts about the tracks of the animals in that family. Take the cards with you when you go on a nature walk and see if you can identify the tracks you find. [Science]

Super Search: Name an animal considered to be a pacer.

On Your Own

mesas, Navaho, sheep herding, Fort Defiance, hogans, Canyon de Chelly, animal tracks, Fort Sumner, The Long Walk, lightning, historical fiction

Suggested Reading

O'Dell, Scott. *The Black Pearl.* Dell/Laurel-Leaf, 1967. Ramon is a young boy who finds a rare black pearl and comes face to face with a deadly sting ray.

————. *Island of the Blue Dolphins.* Houghton, 1960. Karana is forced to live alone on an isolated island off the coast of California for eighteen years. She uses her courage and self-reliance to survive.

————. *Zia.* Dell, 1976. In a sequel to *Island of the Blue Dolphins.* Aunt Karana helps her niece who is being raised in the traditional Indian culture while she tries to deal with the present world of the mission where the girl lives.

Additional Sources

Armstrong, Nancy M., and Paulette Livers Lambert. *Navajo: Long Walk.* The Council for Indian Education. Roberts Rinehart, 1994. Armstrong tells the story of the Long Walk across Arizona and how the Navajo were confined in a camp for four years before they were permitted to return home.

Seasons of a Navajo. Peace River Films, 1986. This 60-minute videocassette was originally shown on television and is a PBS video. It shows one year in the life of an extended Navajo family living on a reservation in the Southwest. It contrasts the traditional life with modern changes.

Sneve, Virginia. *Driving Hawk: The Navajos.* Holiday House, 1993. The book provides an overview of the history and culture of the Navajo Indians.

31

Stone Fox

John Reynolds Gardiner • HarperCollins, 1980
Reading Level: 4.0 • 96 pages

Summary

Little Willy tries desperately to save the family's farm in Wisconsin when his grandfather becomes ill. He enters a dog sledding race hoping to claim the prize money and pay off the back taxes on the farm. A Shoshone Indian, named Stone Fox, and his five powerful sled dogs enter the race. The dogsledding team has won numerous awards in the past and no one believes Little Willy has a chance of winning with his dog, Lightning.

Website Activities

1. Welcome to the State of Wyoming

www.state.wy.us/kids.html

Welcome to the State of Wyoming is a site which contains information about business, government, news, recreation, and attractions in the state of Wyoming.

Activities

Learn about Willy's home state by selecting "Quick Facts About Wyoming" and "All About Wyoming." When you are finished reading these facts, select "Other States Kids' Pages" and locate the website for your home state. Make a chart comparing information for Wyoming and your state. If there is no Web page for your state, search in your classroom or local library for facts. If you live in Wyoming, you may choose any other state for your comparison chart. **[Social Studies]**

Dinosaur fossils and other remains have been found in the state of Wyoming. Select "Dinosaur Quiz Page" and have fun naming the dinosaurs and prehistoric creatures. **[Science]**

Super Search: What is the state dinosaur of Wyoming?

2. Fun 1st: Mr Potato Head

www.fun1st.com/collectors.html

Fun 1st is a marketing, consulting, multimedia, and entertainment company. The company created this fun site on Mr. Potato Head, a registered trademark of Hasbro Toys.

Activity

Little Willy had to find a way to save his grandfather's potato farm. In those days, no one played with potatoes. However, in 1952, Mr. Potato Head was created. Select "The Adventures of Mr. Potato Head" and view the pictures of this remarkable spud as he travels across America. Use the information you learned about Jackson Hole, Wyoming, in *Stone Fox* and from the previous Internet site to draw a picture of Mr. Potato Head dog sled racing in Jackson Hole, Wyoming. **[Art]**

Super Search: Where was Mr. Potato Head born?

3. Samoyed

www.samoyed.org/versatilebeauty.html

Donna Dannen wrote this article entitled: "Samoyed: The Versatile Beauty". She is the president of Organization for the Working Samoyed (OWS).

Activity

Stone Fox had five beautiful Samoyeds pulling his sled. Read this article on Samoyeds and learn why this breed makes good sled dogs and excellent pets. Write five reasons you think Stone Fox raced Samoyeds instead of another breed. Write five reasons why a Samoyed would/would not be a good pet for you.
[Science, Language Arts]

Super Search: What was the name of the first dog to lead an expedition to the South Pole?

4. American Sign Language

dww.deafworldweb.org/asl/

The Deaf World Web created this site which provides the complete dictionary of American Sign Language and other pertinent ASL information.

Activities

Grandfather used a primitive type of sign language to communicate with Willy when he could not speak. Select "Manual Alphabet" and "A to Z." Study the hand and finger positions for the American Sign Language alphabet. Write a comment Willy might have made to Stone Fox after the race. Practice saying this statement in sign language. See if a classmate can understand what you are saying. **[Language Arts]**

Select "Sign Stories" and follow along as you actually get the opportunity to see a story told in sign language. **[Language Arts]**

Super Search: Which letter in sign language is commonly confused with the letter "A"?

5. Storytelling Club

www.storycraft.com

The Kid's Storytelling Club website provides new ideas for telling stories. Each month a new story is created with accompanying crafts and storytelling activities. The site is produced by Storycraft Publishing.

Activity

John Reynolds Gardiner got the idea for *Stone Fox* from a Rocky Mountain legend told to him in 1974. A great storyteller can make a story unforgettable. Select "Create a Story" and learn how to write and tell an exciting story. Choose "Crafts" and "Activities." Use these ideas to help

tell the story. Practice telling the story till you feel comfortable enough to perform the tale for your class. **[Language Arts]**

Super Search: What is the name of the storytelling newsletter available at this site?

On Your Own

potato farming, Wyoming, harmonicas, sign language, dog sleds, winter, taxes, racing dog sleds, Jackson, Wyoming, Samoyeds, Shoshone, Arapaho, Teton mountains, legends

Suggested Reading

Calvert, Patricia. *The Hour of the Wolf.* Scribner, 1983. A loner who cannot please his father is sent to Alaska where he enters the Iditarod Race which is run between Anchorage and Nome.

Gardiner, John Reynolds. *Top Secret.* Bantam, 1984. Allen is determined to do his science project on human photosynthesis and in the process, he becomes green.

Reit, Seymour. *Race Against Death: A True Story of the Far North.* Dodd, Mead, 1976.

Additional Sources

Casey, Brigid, and Wendy Haugh. Sled Dogs. Dodd, Mead, 1983. *Sled Dogs* discusses sled dog breeds, the evolution of the dogs, their uses and sled dog racing.

Costo, Rupert, and Jeannette Henry. *A Thousand Years of American Indian Storytelling.* Indian Historian Press, 1981. This is a collection of 43 traditional tales from a variety of North American Indian tribes.

Stone Fox. Republic Pictures Home Video, 1992. This *Stone Fox* video is a 96-minute video based on the children's book by John Reynolds Gardiner.

32

Summer of My German Soldier
Bette Greene • Bantam Doubleday Dell, 1973.
Reading Level: 5.8 • 198 pages

Summary

The summer that the German POW's come to Arkansas is a memorable one for Patty Bergen. Patty takes a great risk when she shelters an escaped Nazi prisoner. Patty and the young soldier form a special bond but she is forced to pay a price for the role she plays in helping Anton escape.

Website Activities

1. Writing Den

www2.actden.com/writ_den/word.htm

Writing Den is a website designed for students Grades 6–12. The purpose of the site is to help improve English, reading, comprehension, and writing skills.

Activity

Patty used her *Webster's Collegiate Dictionary* to help learn a new word every day. Use this Internet site to sign up for the Word of the Day mailing list. Enter your e-mail address for your class or your home computer. Each day you will be e-mailed a new word and its definition. Be sure to get your teacher's or parent's permission before you sign up for the mailing list. **[Language Arts]**

Super Search: What is the correct spelling for the head or leader of a school?

2. World War II, an American Scrapbook

tqjunior.advanced.org/4616/

This site was created by fifth grade students in Katy, Texas, as an entry in the Think Quest Junior Contest. The students made a World War II American Scrapbook with memories passed down to them from their grandparents and great grandparents.

Activities

Summer of My German Soldier is only one of many stories told of people's experiences during World War II. Read the true recollections of people who lived during the time of the war. The fifth grade students documented these stories and memories told to them from grandparents and relatives about the war and how it changed their lives. Interview your own grandparents, great grandparents, or older family members and collect your data. Write your family's story and make a classroom scrapbook with all of the entries from the members of your class. **[Social Studies, Language Arts]**

Write the recollections Marcy would tell her grandchildren about her experiences during the war. Write the story from Marcy's point of view and have her tell how the decision to help the German soldier affected her life. **[Language Arts]**

Super Search: What is the name of the elementary school where this project was done?

3. FBI Kids' Page

www.fbi.gov/kids/kids.htm

This is the FBI's Kid's and Youth Educational Page on Crime Detection. The publication is devoted to crime detection and crime prevention information.

Activity

The FBI came to Arkansas to investigate the German soldier's escape from the POW camp. In the 1940s, the FBI did not have the techniques in crime detection we have today. Using the information provided at this site, write a few paragraphs explaining how the investigation of Anton's escape would have been different if today's technology had been available to the FBI at that time. **[Science, Language Arts]**

Super Search: What is the name for the acid-carrying coded information which makes every person an individual?

4. Little Explorers

www.littleexplorers.com/languages/ Germandictionary.html

This is an online picture dictionary with definitions, pictures, and website links for words. The dictionaries are available in French, Spanish, German, and Portuguese.

Activity

This Geman-English dictionary would have helped Patty communicate with Anton. Sketch a picture of your classroom and draw objects you would see there —desk, pencil, clock, etc.; Use the Little Explorers dictionary to label each object with the German translation of the words.

[Language Arts, Art]

Super Search: What is the German translation for the object Anton gave Patty when he left?

5. Zig Zag

www.zigzagworld.com/games.htm

Zig Zag Inc. developed this Judaic educational site and uses state-of-the-art computer technology to provide information about the Jewish culture.

Activities

Patty's father was horrified when he learned his Jewish daughter had assisted a Nazi soldier in escaping from the POW camp. The Jewish religion uses the Hebrew alphabet. Click on "Jog Your Memory" and print out the Hebrew alphabet to use when you play the games at this site. Select and play the following Jewish games:

1. Alefbet Go

2. Why Don't Zebras Play Chess?

3. The Hanukkah House

4. A Picnic With Friends

[Social Studies, Language Arts]

Select "Mask and Crown" and learn how to create your own mask and crown for Purim.

[Art]

Super Search: How many letters are in the Hebrew alphabet?

On Your Own

President Franklin D. Roosevelt, Nazis, Victory Gardens, Mississippi River, FBI, Jewish foods, spies, scent dogs, German, physical abuse, Adolph Hitler, Shirley Temple

Suggested Reading

Greene, Bette. *Morning Is a Long Time Coming.* Dial, 1978. Patty is eighteen years old in this sequel to *Summer of My German Soldier.* She is in Paris when she falls in love.

Lowry, Lois. *Number the Stars.* Houghton Mifflin, 1989. During the German occupation of Denmark, Annemarie and her family assist in sheltering her Jewish friend from the Nazis.

Reiss, Johanna. *The Upstairs Room.* Crowell, 1972. A Dutch-Jewish family describes the years spent in hiding from the Nazis during Wold War II.

Additional Sources

Hitler, A Career. RKO Home Video, 1984. This videocassette is based on the book *Hitler,* by Joachim C. Fest and is a film documentary.

Nathan, Joan. *Jewish Cooking in America.* Knopf, 1994. Joan Nathan reviews more than 300 kosher recipes and provides additional information on Jewish dietary laws and traditions.

33
Taking Sides
Gary Soto • Harcourt, Brace, 1991
Reading Level: 5.5 • 138 pages

Summary

Lincoln is the star of his junior high basketball team when his mother makes him move to a safer neighborhood in San Francisco. Now he has to play basketball against his former coach and teammates. He is happy in his new home and is beginning to make friends, but his loyalties still remain with his former buddies.

Website Activities

1. The Locker Room: Sports for Kids!

members.aol.com/msdaizy/sports/bb1.html

The Locker Room: Sports for Kids! is a site which offers sports knowledge, helpful tips, and interesting facts for twelve popular sports played in the USA. It is maintained by S. Poole and has been selected as a "Supersite for Kids" by Bonus.com.

Activity

Lincoln was a star basketball player on his basketball team. Learn more about the history of basketball, rules of the game, fun facts, glossary of terms, and skills and drills for basketball. Use the facts you learned to make a trivia game such as Jeopardy. Write five questions for each of the five categories listed on the Web page. Play the game with your classmates to see which student in your class is the "basketball expert." **[Health]**

Super Search: Who invented the game of basketball?

2. National Crime Prevention Council

www.ncpc.org/

The National Crime Prevention Council is a national nonprofit organization whose mission is to help America prevent crime and build safer, stronger communities. This site is the On-Line Resource Center for the NCPC.

Activities

Even when Lincoln and his mother moved to what they thought was a safer neighborhood, they became the victims of a crime. Select "Children." Have fun learning how to stay safe with these games, tips, and activities. **[Health]**

Select "Teens" and learn "12 Things You Can Do" to stop school violence and make your school a safer place. Discuss the twelve ideas at this site in your classroom and select one of the ideas or create one of your own. Follow through with this idea and work together with your classmates to make your school a safer place. **[Health]**

Select "En Español." Lincoln would be able to read the information on this page. If you have any Mexican-American or Spanish-speaking students in your class, ask them to translate the information from Spanish to English for you. **[Language Arts]**

Super Search: What is the name of McGruff's little buddy?

3. How to Choose the Best Multicultural Books

www.scholastic.com/instructor/curriculum/ langarts/reading/multicultural.htm#soto

This is an article taken from *Instructor Magazine* written for teachers on "How to Choose the Best Multicultural Books." The contributors of the article are Luther B. Clegg, Etta Miller, Bill Vanderhoof, Gonzalo Ramirez, and Peggy K. Ford.

Activities

Gary Soto was raised in a Mexican-American neighborhood in California. He is an award-winning author of numerous books for young adults which portray the Mexican-American culture. Read Gary Soto's tips for writing a successful multicultural book and decide whether he followed his own advice when he wrote *Taking Sides*. Write a small paragraph for each of his tips and explain how he used this information in the book. **[Language Arts]**

Taking Sides is considered to be a multicultural book because the characters portray their cultures in the story. Read the summaries of the multicultural books suggested by Instructor Magazine and choose one book you think you would enjoy reading from each of the five ethnic groups in the list. Tell why you chose these particular books. **[Language Arts]**

Super Search: What is the title of another book written by Gary Soto?

4. The Hummingbird Website

www.portalproductions.com/h/17.htm

This site was designed and is maintained by Larry and Terrie Gates, owners and managers of Portal Productions. The site provides a wealth of information about hummingbird facts, legends, species, migration, *etc.*

Activity

Lincoln was looking outside at his garden when a hummingbird dipped and hovered at the feeder. There are seventeen species of hummingbirds in the United States. View the descriptions of the hummingbirds and take note to the locations of each species on the map locator. Make a list of the names of the hummingbirds which could be found in the San Francisco area of California. Tell which species Lincoln would not have seen in this area of the United States. When you are finished with this activity, return to the home page for more fascinating information on hummingbirds. **[Science]**

Super Search: How far north does the Rufus Hummingbird migrate?

On Your Own

Spanish, Mexican Americans, basketball, graphic artists, eucalyptus, aikido, Mexican foods, rap music, venison, crime statistics, hummingbirds, prejudice, ethnicity in America

Suggested Reading

Soto, Gary. *Baseball in April*. Harcourt, Brace, Jovanovich, 1990. *Baseball in April* is a collection of eleven short stories of Hispanic young people and their adventures growing up in California.

Soto, Gary. *Boys at Work*. Bantam Doubleday Dell, 1995. Rudy and his friend Alex try to find a way to raise money to replace a Discman Rudy broke.

Soto, Gary. *Too Many Tamales*. Putnam, 1993. Maria is horrified when she realizes she lost her mother's wedding ring. She had tried it on when she was making tamales for a family Christmas party.

Additional Sources

Gomez, Paolo. *Food in Mexico*. Rourke, 1989. *Food in Mexico* is one in a series of international food books. It surveys food products, customs, and preparation tips for a variety of Mexican meals.

San Francisco, The Golden Gateway. International Video Network, 1990. This 50-minute travel film of San Francisco is available in VHS and Laser Disc format.

34

A Taste of Blackberries
Doris Buchanan Smith • Thomas Y. Crowell, 1973
Reading Level: 5.0 • 64 pages

Summary

A young boy is with his best friend when the friend is stung by a bee and develops an allergic reaction. The boy has to come to terms with the death of his friend. His family helps him to deal with the grief.

Website Activities

1. Hurst's Berry Farm

www.hursts-berry.com/ssnchrt.html

Hurst's Berry Farm is a wholesale supplier of fresh specialty berries. The company is located in Sheridan, Oregon, and created this site to provide nutritional information and facts about berries.

Activities

The boys enjoyed picking and eating blackberries in *A Taste of Blackberries*. Look at the "season chart" pictograph for the growing seasons of a variety of berries which are grown in Oregon. Make a quiz of five questions based on the season chart. Give the quiz to a student in your class. Have the student take the quiz. Check the answers and discuss the results with your classmate. **[Science, Social Studies]**

Make your own pictograph using produce grown in your area. Be sure to use pictures to represent the fruits and vegetables on your chart. **[Social Studies]**

Super Search: Which berry has the longest growing season?

2. American Medical Association

www.ama-assn.org/insight/h_focus/nemours

This site is sponsored by the American Medical Association, physicians dedicated to the health of America. The site provides health and fitness information, medical news, and a data collection center.

Activities

Years ago there wasn't much research done on allergic reactions to insect bites. Select "Emergencies and First Aid" and then scroll down the Web page to select "Insect Stings and Bites." Read this article and make a list of the symptoms Jamie had when he experienced an allergic reaction to a bee sting. **[Health]**

Read the information provided on spider bites. Compare the treatments recommended for both bee stings and spider bites. Make a diagram to show how the treatments are the same and how they are different. **[Health]**

Super Search: Which two spiders found in the U.S. are poisonous?

3. B-Eye

cvs.anu.edu.au/andy/beye/beyehome.html

Andrew Giger developed this site called to present his research on how a honey bee sees the world.

Activity

Discover how honey bees see the world. Select "Description" and read the scientific explanation of how a bee-eye views objects differently than a human eye. Select "Gallery" and view the patterns and pictures through a bee's eye. Based on the information you learn, sketch a pattern and draw the same pattern from a bee's field of vision.

Super Search: How many dimensions does a bee's vision use?

4. Bibliotherapy

www.noble.mass.edu/nobchild/biblio.htm

This website is a list of children's books which is grouped according to specific problems a child may have. The list is a composite of ideas from twelve librarians on Boston's North Shore.

Activity

Bibliotherapy is the use of books to help children with problems. When Jamie died in the story, the little boy had to deal with issues of death and the grieving process. *A Taste of Blackberries* is suggested on this list under the "Death of a Friend" section. Read the brief summaries for some of the other books which appear on the list. Choose a book you think may have helped you at a special time in your life when you had a problem. Write a few paragraphs describing why you selected this particular book. **[Language Arts]**

Super Search: Name one book on this list which you have read.

5. Popsicle

www.popsicle.com/popsicles/index.html

Good Humor-Breyers Ice Cream sponsors this cool Popsicle site which contains games, contests, and freebies.

Activity

The little boy in *A Taste of Blackberries* was permitted to have one Popsicle a day. Select "Popsicle, Popsicle, Popsicle" and read the facts, riddles, and jokes about Popsicles. Select "Games and Stuff" and then "Construction Zone." Print a pattern, add Popsicle sticks, and you will have your own sailboat, spaceship, fan, or stick people. **[Art]**

Super Search: When was the first Popsicle made?

On Your Own

blackberries, friendship, ALA Notable Books, Japanese beetles, hitchhiking, Morse Code, bee stings, allergic reactions, butterflies, angels

Suggested Reading

Nystrom, Carolyn. *Emma Says Goodbye:* A Child's Guide to Bereavement. Lion Publishing, 1990. Emma comes to terms with her aunt's illness after the aunt is diagnosed with cancer.

Smith, Doris Buchanan. *Best Girl.* Viking, 1993. Young Nealy Compton seeks solace beneath her neighbor's porch when she has difficulties with her mother.

Udry, Janice May. *Let's Be Enemies.* E.M. Hale, 1961. Maurice Sendak illustrates this story of a special friendship between two boys.

Additional Sources

Corr, Charles A., Donna M. Corr, and Clyde M. Nabe. *Death and Dying, Life and Living.* Brooks-Col, 1997. The authors provide an indepth look at how death, dying, and bereavement experiences have shaped our culture. They offer practical guidelines for individuals and families who are coping with grief.

Rofes, Eric. *The Kid's Book About Death and Dying / By and for Kids.* Little, Brown, 1985. Eric Rofes is the editor and coordinator of this collection of facts and advice given by fourteen children who offer a better understanding of death.

Talking with Young Children about Death. PBS Video, 1986. Mister Rogers is featured on this 30-minute VHS recording. The hosts discuss how to approach the subject of death with children.

35

Thank You, Jackie Robinson
Barbara Cohen • Scholastic; 1974
Reading Level: 4.0 • 128 pages

Summary

Sam is a young white boy who can remember details and statistics of every baseball game since history was recorded. Davy is an older black man who faces the racial prejudices of the 1940s. Their love for the Brooklyn Dodgers brings these two unlikely friends together to form a special bond.

Website Activities

1. Jackie Robinson Interview

www.inthegardenstate.com/unionmedia/robinson/Intro.htm

Comcast Online Communications in association with the Institute for Learning Centered Education presents this interview recorded with Jackie Robinson.

Activity

Read the text of an interview Jackie Robinson gave to two journalism students in 1962. You can even hear the actual interview by downloading audio clips to your computer. After listening/reading the interview, list ten new details you learned about Jackie Robinson's life. Check with your teacher or parent before you download any files to your computer. **[Social Studies]**

Super Search: Which former president did Jackie Robinson support?

2. Major League Baseball

www.majorleaguebaseball.com/nbl/

This is the official site of Major League Baseball. The site is maintained by Major League Baseball Enterprises, Inc.

Activity

Read about the history, teams, and players of the Negro Baseball League. View a video clip of Jackie Robinson's legendary swing that made him famous. When you have visited all areas of this site, take the "Negro Leagues Quiz" in the "History" section to see how much you have learned. Please check with your teacher before you download video clips. **[Social Studies]**

Super Search: In which year was the first official recorded appearance of a black baseball team in competition?

3. National Baseball Hall of Fame and Museum

www.baseballhalloffame.org/

The contents of this site are protected and owned by the National Baseball Hall of Fame and Museum, Inc; in Cooperstown, New York.

Activities

Take a virtual field trip to the Cooperstown Hall of Fame. Create a visitor's brochure including important information about hours, admission fees, exhibits, etc. **[Art]**

After visiting the exhibits and features offered at the Hall of Fame, choose three things you would like to see at the Hall of Fame and tell why you chose them. **[Language Arts]**

Super Search: What is the percentage of Major League Baseball players who have been enshrined in the Baseball Hall of Fame?

4. Ball Parks

www.ballparks.com

This website is a collection of details used to describe ball parks and stadiums for the following sports: baseball, basketball, football, and hockey.

Activity

Sam and Davy spent many happy days at Ebbets Field. Click on the picture of the baseball field. Select "National League," "Past," and then "Ebbets Field." Find the dimensions of the field. Select the National or American field which is located closest to your hometown. Draw sketches for Ebbets Field and the field you chose. Write the dimensions of the fields on each of the sketches. Make comparisons between the fields. **[Math]**

Super Search: How many times did the Brooklyn Dodgers win the World Series while playing on Ebbets Field?

5. Biography.com

www.biography.com

The Arts and Entertainment Television Network produces this site containing an Online Database of biographies for over 20,000 personalities.

Activities

Bio-Bytes are original, one-minute documentaries on great lives from the past and present. Select one of the featured bio-bytes and view a video clip of the biography. You will need to have "Real Player" downloaded to your computer to view the clip. **[Social Studies]**

Create your own bio-byte by using a cassette recorder and taping biographical information on a celebrity of your choice. **[Language Arts]**

Super Search: Name one other educational site developed by Arts and Entertainment.

6. Math Baseball

www.funbrain.com/math/

PM Publishing maintains this educational page called Math Baseball.

Activity

Practice your math facts and have fun while you are playing baseball on the computer. You may pick addition, subtraction, multiplication, or division and you may also choose a level of play. **[Math]**

Super Search: How do you enter your answer to the problem?

On Your Own

Ebbets Field, Jackie Robinson, *Pee Wee Reese*, Negro baseball league, civil rights, baseball, Brooklyn Dodgers, Cooperstown Hall of Fame, Major League Baseball

Suggested Reading

Lord, Bette Bao. *In the Year of the Boar and Jackie Robinson.* Cornerstone Books, 1984. A ten-year-old girl emigrates to America in 1947. She really becomes Americanized when she discovers the Brooklyn Dodgers and Jackie Robinson.

Slote, Alfred. *The Trading Game.* Harper Trophy, 1992. Andy makes interesting discoveries about his father and he learns that his grandfather played professional baseball.

Strasser, Todd. *Rookie of the Year.* Trump Club, 1993. Henry dreams of becoming a Chicago Cubs baseball player but he can't even make his high school baseball team.

Additional Sources

Farr, Naunerle C. *Babe Ruth: Jackie Robinson.* Pendulum Press, 1979. This book presents the lives and careers of Babe Ruth and Jackie Robinson in comic strip form.

The Jackie Robinson Story. A William Joseph Heineman Presentation, Xenon Home Video, 1991. This videocassette release of the 1950 motion picture is a biographical story of Jackie Robinson's life and role in baseball. The recording is in black and white in VHS format and is 76-minutes long.

Robinson, Jackie. *Breakthrough to the Big League: The Story of Jackie Robinson.* Cavendish/Grey Castle Press, 1991. The first black baseball player to be accepted by a major league team tells his own story in this autobiography of Jackie Robinson.

36

The War with Grandpa
Robert Kimmel Smith • Bantam Doubleday Dell, 1984
Reading Level: 4.5 • 160 pages

Summary

When his wife dies and he is left alone, Grandpa comes to live with the family and moves into Peter's room. Peter is forced to move all of his belongings to the attic and surrender his room. Peter wages war against Grandpa by playing nasty tricks on him and then Grandpa begins to retaliate with some tricks of his own.

Website Activities

1. Toona Cat's Kids Club

www.toonacat.com/kids/writing/writfram.html

Toona Cat's Kids Club is an award winning website produced by Laurie Hansen. It is a creative place for kids to learn how to write and draw.

Activities

Peter enjoyed making his own book. He preferred writing "lots of chapters that are teeny tiny." Select "Story Map" and learn how a story map can help you to "map out" the structure of great stories before you write a story. You can select an online story map to try out your ideas or a blank story map you can print out to fill in your ideas by hand. When you finish your story, submit it to Toona Cat and it will be placed in the Kid's Club. You may win a Toona Cat T-shirt made especially for you. Make sure to check with your teacher before you submit your story. **[Language Arts]**

Select "Read Stories" and then select "The Adventures of Toona Cat." You have the opportunity to vote on what happens next in the story by submitting your ideas on the website. Check back in a few weeks to see what happens next in the story. **[Language Arts]**

Super Search: What is another name for a complete story idea?

2. Genealogy for Kids

www.geocities.com/EnchantedForest/5283/genekids.htm

Catherine Green explains genealogy to children at this site and tells how to start gathering information for a family tree.

Activity

Peter and his grandfather became great friends in the story. Grandpa shared family stories with Peter. Genealogy is the history of you and your family. Read the information at this site on genealogy and learn how to track down details to help you build your Family Tree. Collect enough data on your family members so that you can complete a chart for three generations in your family. This would include your grandmothers and grandfathers. **[Social Studies, Language Arts]**

Super Search: In the 1800s, where did families record births, marriages, and deaths?

3. Genealogy for Children

home.istar.ca/~ljbritt/

This site is written by Liana Brittain, an elementary teacher. She provides activities for children, links to other genealogy sites, and a list of resources.

Activity

Read the entire page on how people used signs to let others know what they did for a living because they did not know how to write. Make a sign for either Grandpa or Peter's father. Use the information you learned in the story to help you decide which pictures you will draw on your sign. **[Art]**

Super Search: How did people sign documents when they could not write their names?

4. Learn2.com

www.learn2.com/04/0442/0442.html

Learn2.com calls itself the Ability Utility. This site teaches you things that make life easier and/or more interesting.

Activity

Grandpa taught Peter how to clean a fish in the story. Read this set of step-by-step instructions on how to clean a fish. Think of a skill you could share with your classmates. Make an instruction booklet for the skill. Include at least four steps and pictures to illustrate each step. **[Art, Language Arts]**

Super Search: Where are the pectoral fins located on a fish?

5. Rainy Day Playhouse

www.pen-web.com/rainyday/

Rainy Day Playhouse invites kids of all ages to visit this site and have fun playing games and participating in activities. The site was designed by PenWeb Services.

Activities

Peter enjoyed playing board games. Select "Arcade Games" and choose from a large selection of fun and exciting online board games to play. **[Language Arts]**

Select "Puzzles, Strategies, and Word Games" and use your thinking skills to solve these activities. **[Language Arts]**

Super Search: What type of browser is required to play the activities at this site?

On Your Own

grandparents, writing a book, baseball cards, games, accountant, carpenter, emphysema, genealogy, fishing

Suggested Reading

Levison, Riki. *Grandpa's Hotel.* Orchard Books, 1995. A young girl describes the terrific summer she has when she stays at her grandparents' house in the mountains.

Smith, Robert Kimmel. *Chocolate Fever.* Putnam, 1972. Henry breaks out in brown bumps when he eats too much chocolate. He runs away from home and is kidnapped by hijackers who teach him a valuable lesson.

Smith, Robert Kimmel. *Jelly Belly.* Dell, 1981. Jelly Belly is being tormented in his fifth grade class because he is the fattest kid in the school. He wants to lose weight but he is afraid he will starve.

Additional Sources

Family Gathering: Bring Your Family Tree to Life. Palladium Interactive, Commsoft, 1996. This interactive multimedia program contains one computer laser optical disc, one manual, and one guide to online operation. The software provides direct links to genealogy sites on the Internet and helps families to create genealogy charts, journals, multimedia shows, reports, and mailing lists.

Generations Deluxe Edition. Sierra Home, 1998. This CD-ROM software has innovative and flexible charting capabilities to make it possible to produce personalized family history charts.

37

The Watsons Go to Birmingham – 1963
Christopher Paul Curtis • Scholastic, 1995
Reading Level: 5.2 • 224 pages

Summary

Ten-year-old Kenny lives in Flint, Michigan, with his parents and his brother and sister. Kenny's parents decide to take the family on a trip to Birmingham, Alabama, to visit Grandma. His parents hope Grandma may help to "straighten out" Kenny's brother who is an official juvenile delinquent. The Watson family is shocked when they encounter racial bigotry during the heat of the civil rights movement in Alabama in 1963.

Website Activities

1. Sixteenth Street Church

www.16thstreet.org

The Sixteenth Street Church in Birmingham, Alabama, created this website in an effort to more accessible to people who may never have an opportunity to visit Birmingham.

Activity

 The characters and events in Christopher Paul Curtis's novel are fictional but are based on actual events in history. In his epilogue, the author describes the September 15, 1963, incident at the Sixteenth Avenue Baptist Church when four young teenage girls were killed in a bombing. Select "History" and read this historical record of the Sixteenth Street Baptist Church and the bombing incident. In your own words, describe the historical significance of this event and its impact on the civil rights movement. **[Social Studies, Language Arts]**

Super Search: When did the church officially become known as the 16th Street Baptist Church?

2. Internet African-American History Challenge

www.brightmoments.com/blackhistory/

Internet African -American History Challenge is an interactive quiz on important African Americans from the past.

Activity

Read the profiles of important nineteenth-century African Americans. Take the Internet African-American History Challenge to test your knowledge. **[Social Studies]**

Super Search: What was the name of the woman who helped over 200 slaves escape to freedom?

3. Traveling with Kids

travelwithkids.miningco.com

Teresa Plowright created this set of links for Traveling with Kids. She recommends "Games on the Go" which is an article written by Susan Fox for Family Fun Magazine. It contains great ways to pass the time when you are traveling with children in a car on a family trip.

Activity

Mrs. Watson planned the car trip to Birmingham, Alabama. Select "How to Travel with Kids" and "Car Trips: Games on the Go." Read the following sections of the article:

1. Classic Games

2. Backseat Games

3. Tray-top Games

4. Scavenger Hunts

Use an empty shoebox to create a "Backseat Survival Kit" for the next time you travel in a car. Make an index card for each of the games at this site. Write the directions for the games on the index cards and put all of the materials needed to play the games in the shoebox. Be sure to include paper, pencils, crayons, etc; When you are finished, decorate your survival kit and place it in the trunk of your family car so it is ready to use when you need it on your next travel trip. **[Art]**

Super Search: What are "Tray-top Games"?

4. National Civil Rights Museum

www.midsouth.rr.com/civilrights/

This is the home page for the National Civil Rights Museum in Memphis, Tennessee.

Activity

Take a virtual tour of the National Civil Rights Museum in Memphis, Tennessee. The museum is located at the Lorraine Motel where Dr. Martin Luther King was assassinated on April 4, 1968. Start with the "Brown vs. Board of Education of Topeka" exhibit and continue in chronological order until you have visited all of the exhibits. List some of the historical events you feel led up to the 1963 event in Birmingham when the four young girls were killed in the church bombing. **[Social Studies]**

Super Search: When did the national Civil Rights Museum open?

5. Coretta Scott King Honor Award

www.ala.org/srrt/csking/index.html

The American Library Association maintains this site which promotes the highest quality of library and information services on the Internet.

Activity

Christopher Paul Curtis received the Coretta Scott King Honor Award in 1996 for his book

The Watsons Go to Birmingham – 1963. The Coretta Scott King Award honors "African American authors and illustrators for outstanding contributions to children's and young adult literature that promote understanding and appreciation of the culture and contribution of all people to the realization of the American Dream." Select "Coretta Scott King Award Purpose and Criteria." Write a few paragraphs explaining how Christopher Paul Curtis's book meets each of these criteria by giving examples from the book. **[Language Arts]**

Super Search: Who was the first winner of the Coretta Scott King Award?

On Your Own

Coretta Scott King, Sugar Ray Robinson, welfare food, angels, traveling, car games, whirlpools, nicknames, Civil Rights, lazy eye, Martin Luther King

Suggested Reading

Johnson, Angela. *Toning the Sweep.* Scholastic, 1994. Grandmother Ola is dying of cancer and Emmie listens to her stories about the past and learns of her African-American heritage.

Additional Sources

Dubovoy, Sina. *Civil Rights Leaders.* Facts on File, 1997. Sina Dubovoy chronicles the lives of nine civil rights leaders in our country.

Jackson, Jesse and Elaine Landau. *Black in America: A Fight for Freedom.* H. Messner, 1973. This is the history of blacks in America from their beginnings as slaves through troubled times up to the present.

38

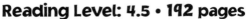

The Wish Giver
The Tales of Coven Tree
Bill Brittain • Harper and Row, 1983
Reading Level: 4.5 • 192 pages

Summary

Four people wander into a shabby old tent at the Coven Tree Church Social and they find a strange little man who gives each one of them a magic card. The weird man disappears and the story becomes fascinating as each person discovers that wishes really do come true if the magic card is used.

Website Activities

1. Make-A-Wish Foundation

www.wish.org/index.html

This is the home page for the Make-A-Wish Foundation of America. The foundation exists to fulfill the special wishes of children under the age of 18 who have life-threatening illnesses.

Activities

Select "FAQ" to find the answers to the most frequently asked questions about the Make-A-Wish Foundation. Create a plan for a fundraising project for your classroom. List the following specifics:

1. What service would you provide to raise money?

2. How many people would need to help you with your project?

3. What is your goal?

4. How long would the project take to complete?
[Language Arts]

Select "How to Donate" and learn how you can become a "Wish Giver" by making a donation or by volunteering your time. Find the address of your local chapter of the Make-A-Wish Foundation and write to the chapter for more information. [Language Arts]

Super Search: How much does the average nationwide wish cost per child?

2. In Step With Idioms

tqjunior.advanced.org/4382/idiom.html

Think Quest Junior is a program which encourages students in grades 4–6 to work together in teams to build Web-based educational materials. This particular Web page is a lesson on idioms developed by 6th graders at Grahamwood Elementary School in Memphis, Tennessee.

Activity

Writers often use idioms to make their stories more colorful and creative. Henry Piper turns into a tree when Rowena uses the following idiom in her wish: "I wish Henry Piper would put down roots." Read "In Step with Idioms" and test your knowledge of idioms by taking the idiom quiz.
[Language Arts]

Super Search: What is another term which means the same as idiom?

3. Tongue Twisters

www.cbc4kids.ca/general/kids-club/tongue-twister/current/default.html

The Canadian Broadcasting Company created this website specifically for kids. Public speakers or people in the communications business practice tongue twisters to help them speak clearly. The CBC developed this tongue twister activity for children.

Activities

Miss Morasco made Polly recite "Peter Piper picked a peck of pickled peppers." Practice the tongue twisters provided at this site. If you have a favorite tongue twister, send it to the Canadian Broadcasting Company and your "twister" might appear on their website. Make sure you check with your teacher before you send your twister. **[Language Arts]**

Select "link" to the site with additional tongue twisters. Make a card game using 3" x 5" index cards. Write a different tongue twister on each card. Shuffle the cards and pass them out so each student in your class receives a card. Allow time for your classmates to practice their "twisters." Collect the cards. See how many students can correctly repeat their tongue twister from memory. **[Language Arts]**

Super Search: Name the other language which is used at this site.

4. Salem Witch Museum

www.salemwitchmuseum.com/

The Salem Witch Museum Site has been selected by the History Channel as a recommended site for children.

Activities

The setting of *The Wish Giver* is Coven Tree in New England. Coven Tree got its name from the trees where groups of witches used to meet. Read the frequently asked questions and the information about the witch trials. Use this information to create a mock witch trial in your classroom. Write a script for your classmates, assign the roles, and have them perform their parts. **[Social Studies, Language Arts]**

Select "1692 Tour" and visit the historical sites where witchcraft events took place. Look on a map of the New England states in the northeastern United States and locate three of the sites mentioned on these Web pages. **[Social Studies]**

Super Search: What was the name of the first witch to be tried in Salem?

On Your Own

magic, witches, New England, good/bad manners, idioms, dowsers, wishes, snake eyes, tongue twisters, traveling

Suggested Reading

Brittain, Bill. *All the Money in the World*. Harper and Row, 1979. Quentin is given his wish for all the money in the world. He also receives a pack of troubles.

Brittain, Bill. *Devil's Donkey*. Harper and Row, 1981. Danil Pitt doesn't believe in magic until he meets Old Magda, the witch, and she proves magic really does exist.

Lasky, Kathryn. *Beyond the Burning Time*. Scholastic, 1994. Twelve-year-old Mary fights to save her mother from being executed during the witchcraft trials in a small New England village in 1691.

Moore, Inga. *The Sorcerer's Apprentice*. Macmillan, 1989. A sorcerers apprentice tries to practice magic when the master leaves him alone but the apprentice's attempts turn disastrous.

Additional Sources

Burgess, Michael. *Magic and Magicians*. Chicago: Children's Press, 1991. This book for children discusses the past and present of supernatural magic and the magic of illusions.

The Crucible, available online at the Salem Witch Museum website <www.salemwitchmuseum.com/>. This CD-ROM includes the entire text of the play, an interview with the playwright Arthur Miller, and an indepth explanation of the McCarthy hearings. A teacher's guide is included.

Super Search Answer Key

Abel's Island
(1) $.95; (2) beam bridge; (3) fishing line; (4) 2.54 centimeters; (5) 50-80%

Across Five Aprils
(1) Nancy Hanks Lincoln;
(2) Appomattox; (3) Tad;
(4) exclamation; (5) Wilmer McLean

After the Dancing Days
(1) George Washington; (2) Puerto Rico, Philippines, Guam, or the Virgin Islands; (3) The Red Cross; (4) John H. Watson, MD

The Black Stallion
(1) chain letter; (2) for meat and milk;
(3) photosynthesis; (4) Patricia Crane;
(5) colt

Bunnicula
(1) because they don't have to chew their food; (2) Yes, if it is raised with the cat.; (3) It is a sign of welcome to any strangers who need food or shelter.;
(4) Answers will vary; (5) *The Celery Stalks at Midnight*

The Cat Ate My Gymsuit
(1) bread, cereal, rice, and pasta;
(2) over 300,000; (3) Kids Health Best Toy Award; (4) *Under the Blook-Red Sun* by Graham Salisbury; (5) 20–30 minutes three times a week

Catherine, Called Birdy
(1) great hall; (2) avian veterinarian;
(3) 1962; (4) serfs or villeins; (5) 2800 BC

The Cay
(1) braille; (2) stoppers; (3) it sinks;
(4) city water may be contaminated;
(5) on the steps of the Lincoln Memorial in Washington, DC

Charlotte's Web
(1) kalua pig; (2) Head, Heart, Hands, Health; (3) 144; (4) Uppercase;
(5) pleasure wheels

The Chocolate Touch
(1) Greece; (2) Hershey, Pennsylvania;
(3) 6 milligrams; (4) double bass; (5) 1528

The Cricket in Times Square
(1) 1907; (2) matsumushi or Truljalia hibinonis; (3) Carus Publishing Company;
(4) Answers will vary; (5) Eurydice

Dragonwings
(1) "I"; (2) Dec. 17, 1903; (3) 450-700 people; (4) the Chinese; (5) 14;
(6) the pipa

Flat Stanley
(1) Flat Stanley, a journal; (2) Accept

any tuber.; (3) 1-800-STAMP24 or 1-800-782-6724; (4) bridle; (5) five;
(6) Answers will vary.

The Great Brain
(1) Answers will vary.; (2) Vermont;
(3) 1910; (4) Monday

The Great Gilly Hopkins
(1) 10; (2) 4,000; (3) David Paterson, the author's son; (4) 1972; (5) Astra

Hatchet
(1) Answers will vary.; (2) Midway, Meigs; (3) English; (4) onions, dandelions, licorice root, or nettle;
(5) three

Homer Price
(1) contraption; (2) 20 years; (3) the mayor; (4) Answers will vary. Garfield was born June 19, 1978.; (5) peanut butter, chocolate bars, oatmeal, cooked bacon, or raw meat

How to Eat Fried Worms
(1) crop; (2) 10 minutes; (3) hinge;
(4) Kenn Nesbitt; (5) Answer will vary.

The Indian in the Cupboard
(1) Grand Entry; (2) Celery Cola; (3) Eli Parker (Donehogawa); (4) band aid;
(5) head for an underpass

James and the Giant Peach
(1) Felicity; (2) tangle web; (3) Llandaff, South Wales; (4) 1 year and 45 days;
(5) 1934

Like Jake and Me
(1) Caroling; (2) five; (3) The answer depends on the locations of current job openings.; (4) Garland, Texas;
(5) Answers will vary.; (6) The Spartans

Mr. Popper's Penguins
(1) the yellow-eyed penguin; (2) Grades 4-8; (3) 4 feet in width; (4) 440;
(5) narrator; (6) 8,000

My Brother Sam Is Dead
(1) 1 out of every 8; (2) 20 seconds;
(3) 20; (4) Irvin Westheimer

My Side of the Mountain
(1) 36; (2) 9 out of 10; (3) 80%;
(4) 2 flags; (5) choosing your writing supplies

Night of the Twisters
(1) aneroid and mercury; (2) 5 seconds = 1 mile; (3) 10 years; (4) Answers will vary.; (5) Grand Island Airport

Owls in the Family
(1) March; (2) songbirds; (3) stalactites;
(4) *Never Cry Wolf*; (5) $30.00

The Pinballs
(1) four times; (2) Answers will vary.;
(3) Answers will vary.; (4) Gemini;
(5) *Summer of the Swans*

Rascal
(1) blue; (2) tennis, baseball, snorkeling;
(3) Niagara River; (4) Mercury ion clock;
(5) 1896

Ribsy
(1) phone number, rabies tag, and license; (2) 72%; (3) October 2, 1950;
(4) Lee Hunt; (5) feel the door

Sing Down the Moon
(1) 2,000 years ago; (2) every Saturday;
(3) 60%; (4) a Leyden jar or a capacitor;
(5) a porcupine, muskrat, beaver, or mountain beaver

Stone Fox
(1) Triceratops; (2) Pawtucket, Rhode Island; (3) Etah; (4) "s"; (5) *Junior Storyteller*

Summer of My German Soldier
(1) principal; (2) McRoberts Elementary;
(3) DNA; (4) ring (der ring); (5) 22

Taking Sides
(1) James Naismith; (2) Scruff; (3) *Too Many Tamales* or any other book written by Soto; (4) Alaska

A Taste of Blackberries
(1) blueberries; (2) black widow and brown recluse (or violin); (3) two dimensions; (4) Answers will vary.; (5) 1905

Thank You, Jackie Robinson
(1) Richard Nixon; (2) 1867; (3) 1%;
(4) one; (5) HistoryChannel.com and HistoryTravel.com; (6) Hit the "Swing" button

The War With Grandpa
(1) premise; (2) in the family bible;
(3) X or t; (4) on either side of the body;
(5) Java

The Watsons Go to Birmingham –1963
(1) 1884; (2) Harriet Tubman;
(3) Games which can be played with a pen or pencil; (4) September 28, 1991;
(5) Lillie Patterson in 1970

The Wish Giver
(1) $3,000.00--$4,000.00; (2) figure of speech; figurative language; (3) French;
(4) Bridget Bishop

Becoming Familiar with Basic Computer Terminology

When you are surfing the Internet, you may encounter unknown specialized computer terms. Here are some of the computer buzz words you will find in this resource book and on the World Wide Web:

bookmarks: A function which allows you to mark a spot on the World Wide Web so you may easily return to it in the future.

browser: Special software needed for navigating on the Internet. The two most common browsers are Netscape and Microsoft Explorer.

chat: A special forum or conference which allows two or more users to communicate in "live" conversations.

clip art: A series of picture files stored on a disk. They can be clipped and posted into a document.

domain: An address on the Internet to make it easier to locate information without having to remember a long list of numbers or letters. Here are a few common extensions to domains which might appear at the end of a URL (Universal Resource Locator):

  .edu—education
  .gov—government
  .com—commercial
  .net—network
  .mil—military
  .org—nonprofit organization

download: To transfer a file from another computer into your own computer.

DVD: (digital video disc) A high-capacity optical disc used to store computer applications and full-length movies.

e-mail: Short for electronic mail, which is sent across the Internet from one computer to another.

FAQ: (Frequently Asked Questions) Lists created to act as an aid in troubleshooting problems or to provide users with answers to commonly asked questions on a topic.

font: A specific type style; a set of letters, numbers, and other characters having a similar style.

home page: The main introductory page of a website which contains a table of contents and links to other pages on the site or on the World Wide Web.

icon: A small picture used to represent a disk or a file.

Internet: An international network of computers linked together to provide information, e-mail, news, and other services.

laserdisk: A disk recorded with sound and pictures and read by a laser beam.

links: Words or images on a Web page which lead you to other files, pages, or sites on the Internet.

menu: A list of choices.

online: When you are "online," your computer is connected to a host computer which provides you with access to the Internet or another information sources.

Quick-time: A format used to view movie files.

Real audio: A computer program you can use to download and listen to sound files.

search engine: A software program designed to help users locate websites on specific subjects.

Shockwave: A program which provides you with interactive multimedia capabilities for your computer. Shockwave is used to play games at many sites.

snail mail: Regular US Postal mail.

URL: (Universal Resource Locator) An electronic address for a Web page.

virus: A computer program designed to sabotage another program and damage operations on computers.

Web page: The name for a collection of information related to a specific topic.

World Wide Web: A network that provides access to information on the Internet by using multimedia files.

Appendix B

Additional Professional Resources

The following list of materials may be helpful in locating specific websites to integrate the Internet into the curriculum, and may be useful to librarians seeking creative applications of the Internet in youth programs.

Books

Gralla, Preston. *Online Kids: A Young Surfer's Guide to Cyberspace.* John Wiley, 1996. *Online Kids* provides practical information on how to navigate the World Wide Web and lists specific sites in categories which are easily recognized.

Heide, Ann, and Stilborne, Linda. *The Teacher's Complete and Easy Guide to the Internet.* Teacher's College Press: 1997. Heide and Stilborne wrote this guide which includes an introduction to the following components of the Internet: mailing lists, newsgroups, gophers, ftp, and the WWW.

Jasmine, Grace and Jasmine, Julia. *Internet Directory for Teachers.* IDG Books Worldwide, 1997. The book comes with a CD-ROM. Both the book and CD guide teachers to the most useful resources on the Internet and include an Internet service provider, a search engine, and links to sites.

Mandel, Mimi. *Teens Guide to the World Wide Web.* Alleyside Press, 1999. *The Guide* describes over 700 websites of interest to young adults.

Skomars, Nancy. *Education with the Internet: Using Net Resources at School and Home.* Charles River Media, 1997. This book is designed to aid teachers and librarians in integrating the Internet into the classroom. It comes with a CD that includes site listings, lesson plans, and templates for creating Web pages.

Want, Robert S. *How to Search the Web: A Quick Reference to Finding Things on the World Wide Web.* Want Publishing, 1998. The book explains in non-technical terms, how the major search engines work. It is intended for researchers, librarians, journalists, teachers, and students.

Educational Videos

Internet for Educators. Wehman Video Distribution, 1996. This 48 minute video is a step-by-step guide to using and understanding the Internet for teachers and librarians. E-mail, Telnet, gophers, and the World Wide Web are explained and a disk filled with useful WWW sites is included with the video.

The Internet Video. Osprey Film Productions, 1995. This instructional video provides information on accessing and using the Internet.

No-Brain on Internet. Cerebellum, 1998. Practical hints on surfing the Web, transferring files, and using e-mail are given in this 45-minute educational video.

The Video Guide to the Internet. QV Publishing, 1995. This is an instructional video which uses graphics and demonstrations to give an overview of the Internet.

Websites:

Education World
This is the site for educators to gather and share ideas. It's designed to make it easy for educators to integrate the Internet into the classroom by providing lesson plans, articles, and an education search engine with over 100,000 educational sites.

Classroom Connect <www.classroom.net>
Classroom Connect provides online materials and links to thousands of sites for K–12.

Finding Information on the Internet
<www.lib.berkeley.edu/TeachingLib/Guides/Internet/FindInfo.html>
The University of California, Berkley created this tutorial. The tutorial progresses from beginner to advanced surfer.

Kathy Schrock's Guide for Educators
<www.capecod.net/schrockguide/index.htm>
This is a categorized list of sites on the Internet found to be useful for enhancing curriculum and teachers' professional growth.

Surfing the Net with Kids
<www.surfnetkids.com>
This resource for parents, kids, teachers, and librarians lists educational websites in content-area groupings.